YANKEE MAGAZINE'S
GREAT NEW ENGLAND RECIPES

Photographs by — Carole Allen: 14, 24, 36, 42, 48, 64, 74, 114, 164, 244, 262, 294;
Edie Clark: 176; Paul Darling: 92, 94; Joseph Evans: 130; Deborah Karr: 120, 156,
194, 202, 210, 222, 232, 238; Carol McCabe: 138; Nancy Nassiff: 56, 104, 146,
186, 284; Peter Vandermark: 84, 250; Patricia Whitcomb: 270, 278, 304.

Text courtesy of — Mel Allen: 43, 115, 245; Deborah Karr: 233; Susan Mahnke: 15,
25, 37, 49, 57, 75, 85, 93, 105, 147, 157, 165, 177, 187, 195, 203, 211, 223,
251, 263, 271, 285, 295, 305; Carol McCabe: 139, 239; Anita Mortimer: 65;
Barbara Rogers: 121, 131; Patricia Whitcomb: 279.

Yankee Books, a division of Yankee Publishing Incorporated, Dublin, New Hampshire 03444

First Edition

Copyright 1983, by Yankee Publishing Incorporated

Printed in the United States of America

Library of Congress Catalog Card No. 82-51210

ISBN: 0-911658-36-X

YANKEE MAGAZINE'S
GREAT NEW ENGLAND RECIPES
And The Cooks
Who Made Them Famous

YANKEE BOOKS

a division of

Yankee Publishing Incorporated

Dublin, New Hampshire

Table of Contents

MARGUERITE (DIMINO) BUONOPANE — 64

Stuffed Artichokes, Chicken Cacciatore, Lobster Fra Diablo, Lentil Soup, Ravioli, Biscotti, Italian Twists.

ANN CHANDLER — 74

Salsa Picante, Frijoles, Sopa de Arroz, Chilaquilles, Chalupas, Tostados, Chandler Chili, Louisiana Red Beans and Rice, Sopapillas.

PATTI COFFEY — 84

Chicken Liver Pâté, Lobster Quiche, Scalloped Oysters Cormier, Tourtière, Apple Pie, Pecan Pie, Pie Crust, French Cheesecake, Myriah's Apricot Brandy.

SUSIE CROSS — 92

How To Make Hand-Dipped Chocolates, Buttercream Centers, Peanut Butter Squares, Meltaways, Coconut Chocolate Meringue Bars, Chocolate Buttersweets, Ischler Cookies, Sugar Cookie Cutouts, Frosted Shortbreads.

KATHLEEN DONOHUE — 104

Finnish Braid, Raisin Bread, Sunny Acres Corn Chowder, Kabisuppe, Mushrooms à la Grecque, Spinach Lasagna, Cream Cheese Foldovers, Chocolate Pudding, Chilled Chocolate Loaf, Blue Ribbon Pumpkin Pie.

AVIS DUDLEY — 114

Italian Dressing, Baked Brown Potatoes, Stuffed Baked Potatoes, Dean's Brownies.

PAT ESTEY — 120

Lemon Bread, Apricot-Cranberry Loaf, Applesauce Nut Bread, Pumpkin Bread, Sweet Roll Dough, Christmas Stollen.

CAROLE EVANS — 130

Vegetable Casserole, Papa's Lamb with Orzo, Mother's Lemon Baked Chicken, Moussaka, Easter Bread, Koulourakia.

DOROTHY FOLSOM — 138

Seafood Newburg, Cream Puffs, Raspberry Cocoa Ice Cream, Spice Cake, Meringue Cake, Fudge Pie, Cinnamon Sticks, Apple Crisp for 60.

JUDY GORMAN — 146

Baked Stuffed Mushrooms, Crostini di Ricotta e Salsiccie, Gnocchi Verde, Scampi, Scaloppine di Maiale, Zucchini and Tomato Casserole, Tortoni, Chocolate Mousse.

MABEL GRAY — 156

Beignets Soufflés, Oatmeal Bread, Pocketbook Rolls and Cinnamon Buns, Zucchini Soup, German Baked Beans, Gingerbread, Eleanor's Bakeless Chocolate Cookies, Mother's Squash Pie.

BRUCE JOHNSON — 164

Manhattan-Style Clam Chowder, Apple Butter, Red Cabbage, Chicken à la Russe, Tarragon Chicken, Veal Ragout, German Pot Roast, Beef Stroganoff, Spaetzle, Nüsstorte.

CARLA (FERRY) KARDT — 176

Swedish Rye Bread, Irish Soda Bread with Caraway, Italian Vegetable Soup, Midwestern Chowder, Marinated Fish with Sour Cream, Three's-A-Crowd Omelet, Leek and Herb Quiche, Marinated Mushrooms and Green Beans, Lemon-Orange Mousse.

JURIS KUPRIS — 186

White Bread, Whole-Wheat Honey Bread, Raisin Bread Braids, Apple Whole-Wheat Honey Squares, Piragi, Piparkukas.

JUDY LUND — 194

Breakfast Pancake, Quick Orange-Yogurt Coffee Cake, Tomato Consommé, Chutney Puffs, Roast Goose, Goose Stuffing, Plum Pudding, Dark Plum Duff.

CORINNE MORSE — 202

Swedish Pastry, Watermelon Pickle, Feta Cheese Appetizers, Zucchini Soup, Corn Pudding, Seafood Casserole, Latvian Torte, Strawberry Glaze Pie.

MILLIE NELSON — 210

Assorted Vegetable Dish, Stir-Fried Snow Peas, Fish with Sweet-Sour Sauce, Meat-Vegetable Dumplings, Shredded Vegetables and Beef, Lion's Head Meatballs, Swedish Cardamom Coffee Bread, Rye Bread, Dinner Rolls, Brysell Cookies, Rhubarb Pudding.

SHIRLEY OLADELL — 222

Two-Cabbage Slaw, Corn Pudding, Carrot Casserole, Sweet Potato and Pineapple Casserole, Hot Chicken Salad, Skillet Chicken Tetrazzini, Refrigerator Bran Muffins, Pioneer Bread Pudding, Rich Strawberry Shortcake, Strawberry Pie Platter with Orange Sauce.

DOROTHY OLIVEIRA — 232

Chicken Fricassee, Old-Fashioned Drop Cookies, Blueberry Slump, Indian Pudding, Pompadour Pudding.

DOROTHY RATHBUN — 238

Wickford Clam Chowder, Jonny Cakes, Moist Oatmeal Bread, White Bread, Molasses Whole Wheat Bread, Peanut Butter Fudge.

NELLIE REED — 244

Chicken Pie, Pie Crust, Baked Stuffed Haddock, Seafood Casserole, Molasses Cookies, Molasses-Blueberry Cake.

BARBARA RILEY — 250

Homemade Peanut Butter Granola, Strawberry-Rhubarb Muffins, Calcutta Indian Bread, Mustard à la Maison, Homemade Crackers, Quatre Épices, Onion Pie, Lasagna Roll-Ups, Banana Tart.

HELEN & BERTHA ROBB — 262

Robb Farm Frosty, Helen's Doughnuts, Helen's Pancakes, Maple Mountains, Maple Bran Muffins, Maple Oatmeal Muffins, Graham Bread, Marjorie Thurber's Home-Baked Beans, Sweet Potato-Maple-Apple Casserole, "My Bread Pudding," Poor Folks' Plum Pudding.

MILDRED PRESTON & JANICE PRESTON STAFFORD — 270

Cranberry Salad, Jeanne Dube's Walterspiel, Mildred's Chowder, Betty Rand Bassett's Spinach Bars, Pat Heinrich's Mustard Sauce, Jetta Swiat's Chicken Divan, Harriet Riggs' Date Cookies, Mildred's Raspberry Pie.

MARION & ADA URIE — 278

Marion's Scandinavian Rolls, Cottage Cheese Dill Bread, Ada's Carrot Casserole, Ada's Baked Indian Pudding, Marion's Raspberry Pie, Marion's Maple Butternut Fudge.

HILDUR WEEDEN — 284

Baked Beans; Roast Chicken, Turkey, Beef, Lamb, or Pork; Cream Puffs; Old-Fashioned Raisin-Filled Cookies; Spritz Cookies; Brownies; Old-Fashioned Rice Pudding; Halloween Fudge; Fluffy Sponge Cake; Gingerbread.

SUE WELLWOOD — 294

Granola, Tomato Pick-Me-Up, Herb Omelet, Tabouli, Gazpacho, Macaroni Salad, Scallop Salad, Spinach Lasagna, Blueberry Pudding.

FOREWORD

In December of 1977, the headline "Great New England Cooks" appeared in *Yankee* Magazine for the first time, with this explanation: "Their casseroles are always the first to go at church suppers. When a dignitary comes to town they are asked to prepare the meal. Almost every town in New England has one, and from time to time *Yankee* will visit these cooking experts to learn their culinary secrets. If you know a truly exceptional cook, please write and tell us about him or her." Dozens of cooks later, the series is still going strong — mostly because running out of great cooks in this part of the world is about as likely as a maple tree running out of sap, or a hill farmer running out of rocks in his field. Good cooking is just a natural part of New England.

Of course, everyone has his or her own idea of what good food is. Some cooks go strictly by the book, measuring every ingredient carefully, practicing favorite recipes until they are honed to perfection, planning menus down to the last course weeks in advance — and their food is delicious. Other cooks stir in a dash of this, a handful of that, never make a recipe the same way twice, prepare gorgeous meals from what most people would consider a motley collection of leftovers — and *their* food is delicious too!

In the process of doing many of the interviews that this book draws on, I made new friends, enjoyed many good laughs, and, not least of all, tasted some of the best food of my life, everything from the most classic New England baked beans and clam chowder to homemade bagels, Northern Italian gnocchi, and deep-fried wontons. Not that there weren't a few culinary pratfalls along the way.

One cook's oven upped and quit halfway through the interview, and the quick bread she was baking stayed forever at the consistency of pudding. Another time a gremlin in my typewriter changed baking soda to baking powder in a muffin recipe, and the mistake went unnoticed until irate and puzzled readers began writing in to ask why their muffins came out as little cement doorstops. (That's when we began checking and double-checking all of the recipes. Barring another gremlin, we can assure you that these recipes really work: members of our staff here at Yankee Books and I have personally cooked and sampled each and every one!)

I want to thank all the Great New England Cooks I met for the valuable lessons you taught me. You showed me that it's not food processors and fancy French knives that give food a "gourmet" touch (although you all have the Yankee practicality to realize that good equipment and modern conveniences can make a slow job go faster, and in some cases, with better results). You taught me that "gourmet" cooking is really more of an attitude than a certain set of recipes, that cooking anything with care and imagination gives it a gourmet touch. You took standard recipes from cookbooks, the backs of cans and boxes, and your own friends and relatives, and made them uniquely yours with your secret little touches (which I always tried, sometimes without success, to ferret out). Mostly you demonstrated that the one "ingredient" all great cooks have in common is a commitment to preparing good food for your family and friends — one of the myriad forms of love.

Susan Mahnke
Senior Editor, *Yankee* Magazine
June 1982

ROSE ABRAMS
Malden, Massachusetts

Rose Abrams' specialties are a delightful blend of traditional Jewish recipes from her mother and the mainstream New England cooking she learned as a young girl at a neighbor's house in Boston's West End. "It wasn't Jewish cooking — it was American style," says Rose, "but Mother thought it was great — she said I should always be ready to try something new."

Rose is a self-confessed perfectionist when it comes to cooking. "My father always told me, 'If it doesn't turn out right, do it again.' The first time I made a sponge cake, the top crust was like a rock. I threw it out and started over — and it came out fine."

Rose always let her daughter, Rebecca, help out in the kitchen, and now Rebecca's daughter, Heather, is gaining valuable experience from both her mother and grandmother. Enthusiastic and indefatigable (good qualities in a cook), Heather can often be found after school or on weekends at her grandmother's elbow.

Personal variations stamp each dish Rose prepares as her very own. "I look at recipes, and then I diverge a little." And it's those divergences that make her cheesecake a poem to the potentials of cream cheese, her chicken soup a tranquilizer to soothe any beast, her bagels an inspiration to every cook.

REBECCA'S CHICKEN SOUP WITH KNEDL

A fine chicken soup with the added bonus of feather-light knedl (dumplings). Vegetable quantities can be varied to taste.

1 whole chicken, suitable for stewing	Salt to taste
3 onions, chopped	5 chicken bouillon cubes
4 to 5 stalks celery, chopped	Chopped parsley
4 to 5 carrots, sliced	Knedl (recipe follows)

Cover chicken with water and bring to a boil. Skim foam several times, then lower to a simmer and add onions, celery, carrots, salt to taste, and bouillon cubes. Simmer until chicken is tender, about 1 to 1½ hours. Remove chicken, cool, and bone. Return chicken meat to soup and add chopped parsley. Add knedl to simmering soup; serve in shallow soup bowls.

Makes 2 quarts.

KNEDL (Matzo Balls)

2 tablespoons fat, melted	1 teaspoon salt
2 eggs, lightly beaten	2 tablespoons soup stock or water
½ cup matzo meal	

Mix fat and eggs. Add meal and salt; add stock and mix well. Cover and refrigerate for at least 20 minutes (mixture will thicken). Form into balls the size of walnuts and cook in simmering chicken soup, covered, for 30 to 40 minutes.

CHALLAH

"My version is really a rich egg bread. A real challah is made with water instead of milk, and oil instead of butter."

2 packages dry yeast
½ cup warm water
1½ cups lukewarm
　milk
¼ cup sugar
1 tablespoon salt
3 eggs

¼ cup soft butter
7¼ to 7½ cups flour
1 egg yolk
2 tablespoons cold
　water
Poppyseeds (optional)

Dissolve yeast in warm water. Add milk, sugar, salt, 3 eggs, butter, and half the flour. Mix until smooth. Add remaining flour, enough so dough handles easily. Knead, and let rest for 5 minutes. Place in a greased bowl and let rise until doubled. Punch down. To shape loaves, divide dough into 1 small and two large portions. Divide each portion into thirds, and roll each third into a rope. Braid three ropes together, tucking ends under. Let braids rise on a greased cookie sheet, covered, until doubled. Before baking, brush with a mixture of 1 egg yolk and cold water, and sprinkle with poppyseeds if desired. Bake in a preheated oven at 375° for 35 to 45 minutes, until golden brown. Bread will sound hollow when tapped. Cool on racks.

Makes 1 small and 2 large braided loaves.

ROSE'S BAGELS

Even the most timid cook can learn how to make plump, glossy bagels if Rose's directions are followed carefully. For best results, she suggests the following: never let the dough rise too long — twenty minutes at the most; boil the bagels for exactly seven minutes, and in water that has had a spoonful of honey added to it; don't cook too many at a time; and brush bagels with an egg wash partway through the baking.

4 to 5 cups flour
3 tablespoons sugar
1 tablespoon salt
1 package dry yeast
1 egg yolk
1½ cups very warm
   water

1 tablespoon honey
1 egg white, beaten
1 tablespoon cold water
Poppyseeds (optional)

In a large bowl mix together 1½ cups flour, sugar, salt, and yeast. Gradually add egg yolk and warm water, and beat for 2 minutes at medium speed with an electric beater. Add ½ cup more flour and beat at high speed for 2 minutes. With a spoon, stir in enough of the remaining flour to make a soft dough. Turn dough onto a floured board. Knead for 8 to 10 minutes (add more flour if dough is too sticky). Place in an ungreased bowl. Cover, and let rise for 20 minutes (dough will not be doubled). Punch down and turn onto a floured board. Cut into about 10 pieces and roll each piece between your hands to make a rope about 8 or 9 inches long; pinch the ends together to form circles. Place on ungreased baking sheets. Cover and let rise for 20 minutes (not until doubled). In a large shallow pan boil 1¾ inches water. Stir in honey. Lower heat and add a few bagels at a time, being careful not to crowd them. Simmer for 7 minutes, turning bagels over halfway through cooking period. Place on a towel to cool for 5 minutes,

(Cont'd)

then place on ungreased baking sheets. Bake bagels at 375°
for 10 minutes. Remove from oven, brush with a mixture of
egg white and cold water, sprinkle with poppyseeds if desired,
and return to oven. Bake for 20 minutes longer. Cool on wire
racks. Serve split and toasted.   *Makes 10.*

POPPYSEED COOKIES

*Tender, lightly crisp cookies with just a hint of lemon flavor.
Excellent with mid-morning coffee or for an afternoon tea. The
dough is very sticky so flour hands frequently when shaping it
into balls.*

¾ cup oil	4 cups flour
1 cup sugar	2 teaspoons baking
3 eggs	powder
Juice of 1 large lemon	½ cup poppyseeds
1 teaspoon vanilla	

Blend oil and sugar. Add eggs, lemon juice, and vanilla; beat
thoroughly. Sift flour and baking powder and add to sugar
mixture. Stir in poppyseeds. Form dough into balls the size of
walnuts and flatten them with a floured fork until thin. Bake
on greased cookie sheets at 375° for 12 to 15 minutes. Cookies
will remain fairly pale. Cool on racks.   *Makes 4½ dozen.*

CHEESE BLINTZES

Neat little envelopes with rich cheese filling, gently browned in butter. "I cover them with plastic as I make and stack them so they won't dry out. Some recipes use milk in the batter, but I use water — I think it makes them lighter. I use farmer's cheese, but you can substitute well-drained cottage cheese."

Filling:

½ pound cream cheese	2 egg yolks
1 cup cottage cheese	2 tablespoons sugar, or
6 ounces farmer's	more to taste
cheese or well-	Dash of cinnamon
drained cottage	1 tablespoon melted
cheese	butter

Combine all ingredients and mix well. Refrigerate until blintzes are ready.

Blintzes:

3 eggs	¾ cup sifted flour
1 cup water	Oil
½ teaspoon salt	
2 tablespoons melted butter	

Beat eggs with water, salt, and melted butter. Stir in flour. Heat a little oil in a 7- or 8-inch skillet or crêpe pan. Add about 2 tablespoons batter, tilting pan to cover bottom. Make sure batter is thin, and don't use too much oil to grease the pan. Brown blintz on one side only. Flop out of pan onto a clean towel, cooked side up. Cover with plastic and continue to make more blintzes. Do not let blintzes dry out before filling. To fill, place about 1 rounded tablespoon of filling on the cooked surface of a blintz. Fold blintz around filling in an envelope shape and pinch lightly to seal. Fry in butter, and serve hot. *Makes about 10.*

CHEESECAKE SQUARES

A miniature version of cheesecake but so easy to make.

1 cup flour
½ cup brown sugar
6 tablespoons butter
8 ounces cream cheese, softened
¼ cup granulated sugar
1 egg
2 tablespoons milk
¼ teaspoon lemon rind
2 tablespoons lemon juice
2 tablespoons chopped nuts

Combine flour and brown sugar; cut in butter until mixture is crumbly. Set aside 1 cup of mixture and press the remainder into an ungreased 8-inch square pan. Bake at 350° for 12 to 15 minutes. Meanwhile, combine cream cheese, granulated sugar, egg, milk, lemon rind and juice, and beat well. Spread over baked crust. Combine reserved topping with chopped nuts, and sprinkle over cheese mixture. Bake at 350° for 25 minutes. Cool and cut into squares. *Makes 16 squares.*

CHEESECAKE

A rich, fine-textured cheesecake topped with a shimmering glaze of strawberries. Rose's recipe calls for a liberal amount of lemon juice for she feels it offsets the richness of the cream cheese and sour cream and helps lighten the cake's texture. After the cake bakes for one hour, she simply turns off the oven, leaving the cake inside to cool down gradually for another hour or so. Letting it cool off slowly helps prevent the top from cracking. During the final cooling period, she cooks the strawberry topping, then lets it cool enough to spread on top of the cake.

Crust:

1 package plus 4 additional graham crackers, crushed	6 tablespoons butter ⅛ teaspoon vanilla ¼ cup sugar

Rub all ingredients together with your fingers until mixture is blended. In a 10-inch springform pan, pat the crust onto the bottom of the pan, and bring the edges up as far as possible.

Cheese Filling:

1 pound cream cheese 1 cup sugar 6 egg yolks 1 pint sour cream 3 tablespoons lemon juice	Dash of cinnamon 1 teaspoon vanilla 3 scant tablespoons flour 6 egg whites

Cream together cream cheese and sugar. Stir in egg yolks, sour cream, lemon juice, cinnamon, and vanilla. Add flour and stir until blended. Whip egg whites until they hold a peak, and fold in thoroughly. Pour into crust and bake in preheated 300° oven for 1 hour. Then shut off heat and leave cake in oven (keep door closed) for 1 hour longer. Open door and let cake remain in oven 15 minutes more. Cool thoroughly.

Topping:

1 carton (10 ounces)
   frozen strawberries in
   syrup (not fresh-
   frozen in plastic
   pouch)
2 tablespoons
   cornstarch

⅓ cup sugar
½ teaspoon lemon
   rind
1 teaspoon lemon juice

Thaw berries and drain, reserving syrup. In a small pan, mix cornstarch, sugar, lemon rind, and lemon juice, and gradually add ¾ cup strawberry syrup. Cook, stirring constantly, until mixture comes to a boil and clears. Let cool about 7 minutes. Add strawberries and spread topping on cooled cake.

Serves 12-14.

Lib Andrews
Sanbornton, New Hampshire

Lib Andrews has made English muffins for friends and family all around the world — India, Ethiopia, Belgium, Denmark, wherever husband Henry's travels in search of plant fossils took the family — but most of her muffins originated right in her Sanbornton, New Hampshire, kitchen, mixed according to a "secret" recipe Lib got from her sister years ago.

Lib's culinary talents don't stop with English muffins, however. Wherever she has lived she has given classes in gourmet and international cooking, and she has spent a lot of her time just experimenting in her own kitchen. "Not everything you make always turns out perfectly, or the way you expect it to," she says, "but there's an old saying that I tell to all my students: 'The beauty of handwork is its imperfections.' I've always had a lot of encouragement from my husband, Henry, who has been game to try anything. You just can't learn to cook with a meat-and-potatoes man!"

ENGLISH MUFFINS

Lib uses a series of tin cans to cut out her muffins: tomato paste cans for cutting hors d'oeuvre-size muffins, mushroom cans, tuna cans, soup cans. The muffins are baked in ungreased electric skillets on a layer of stone-ground cornmeal that is slowly heated until it gives off an unmistakable nutty odor and begins to brown slightly. (Baking muffins in the oven would make them spherical, not flattened.) She shakes out the browned cornmeal from the skillet and adds a new layer for each batch. Her muffins are light and fragrant, and soft on the inside, with enough nooks and crannies to please any butter addict.

1 cake compressed yeast, or 1 tablespoon dry yeast (1 package)	2 tablespoons sugar
	1¼ teaspoons salt
	½ cup evaporated milk
1 teaspoon sugar	4 cups flour
¼ cup lukewarm water	(approximately)
	1 egg
½ cup boiling water	Cornmeal
3 tablespoons margarine or Crisco shortening	

Dissolve yeast and 1 teaspoon sugar in lukewarm water. Pour boiling water over shortening, 2 tablespoons sugar, and salt; stir to melt shortening. Add milk and cool to lukewarm. Add 2 cups flour and beat until smooth. Add egg and beat well; add dissolved yeast mixture and mix well. Add more flour — just enough to form a moderately stiff dough. Knead until smooth and satiny, then place in greased bowl and turn dough so greased side is up. Cover and set in warm place to rise until doubled in bulk. Punch down; let rest 5 minutes. Roll out on a lightly floured surface to less than ½-inch thickness and cut into 3- or 4-inch rounds. Place on a cookie sheet which has been covered with cornmeal, cover, and let rise until doubled in

(Cont'd)

bulk. Heat an ungreased heavy skillet or frying pan (325° on an electric skillet) covered with a layer of cornmeal until the cornmeal just starts to turn brown. Place the muffins, top side down, on the cornmeal and cook, uncovered, slowly for about 10 minutes, then turn carefully and cook on the other side about 10 minutes, or until done. Cool on rack. Split, toast, and butter to serve (or just split and butter while still warm).

Makes 1-1½ dozen,
depending on size of cutter.

Variations: To make whole wheat English muffins, substitute half whole wheat flour and half unbleached flour for the white flour. The egg may be left out, if desired; 1 tablespoon of wheat germ may be added. About ½ cup of currants or raisins may be added to either type of dough.

(Cont'd)

COACHMAN'S SPECIAL

This is as easy to make as sloppy joes, but much more of a treat.

1 pound lean ground beef	Salt and pepper to taste
Butter or margarine	Mayonnaise
2 tablespoons flour	Chopped sweet onion
1¼ cups consommé or beef bouillon, or 1 can (10½ ounces)	

Brown beef in enough butter or margarine to keep it from sticking. Chop up while cooking to make it crumbly. Add flour and cook a few minutes before adding consommé or bouillon. Stir well and simmer for about 30 minutes. Mixture should be moist, but not runny. Serve hot on split, toasted English muffin halves, and topped with a generous dollop of a mixture of mayonnaise and chopped onion.

Enough for 6-8 English muffin halves.

GWENDOLYN SPECIAL

Perfect for brunch, Sunday supper, or unexpected company — so simple, they can be prepared in a matter of minutes.

¾ pound cheddar cheese, grated	1 green pepper, chopped
½ pound bacon, cooked and cut into bits	Mayonnaise to moisten
	6 to 8 English muffins, toasted

Mix all but last ingredient together and place a heaping tablespoonful on each toasted English muffin half. Heat under a broiler until cheese melts and browns lightly. *Serves 6-8.*

THE UBIQUITOUS CRAB

A milder cheese works just as well in this versatile dish, which can be served as an hors d'oeuvre, turned into a casserole with the addition of a little milk and some cooked rice or pasta, or used as a topping for English muffins or as a filling in rolled fillet of sole.

2 packages (3 ounces each) cream cheese
¾ cup mayonnaise
½ pound sharp cheddar cheese, grated
1 to 2 cups crab meat
1 onion, minced

2 hard-boiled eggs, peeled and finely chopped
¼ teaspoon dry mustard
½ teaspoon paprika
Freshly ground black pepper

Mix cream cheese with mayonnaise until smooth. Add rest of ingredients, mix well, and refrigerate. Use as desired.

Makes about 5 dozen hors d'oeuvres.

HAM LOAF AND MUSTARD SAUCE

A pleasant change from the usual meat loaf. If desired, add a little minced onion before baking. The sauce makes a large amount, and the remainder can be stored in the refrigerator and used as needed.

1 pound ground ham
½ pound ground pork
1 egg, beaten
1 cup milk
1 cup lightly salted
  cracker crumbs
1 small green pepper,
  chopped

¼ cup maple syrup
1 tablespoon dry
  mustard
Mustard Sauce (recipe
  follows)

Mix first 6 ingredients together, reserving a few pieces of green pepper, and place in a greased loaf pan. Top with the green pepper pieces and bake at 350° for 1 hour, 10 minutes. During the last 20 minutes, baste with the maple syrup mixed with the dry mustard. Serve with Mustard Sauce.   *Serves 4-6.*

MUSTARD SAUCE

1½ cups Dijon
  mustard
4 teaspoons dry
  mustard
¾ cup sugar

½ cup white vinegar
1⅓ cups oil
1 cup chopped fresh
  dill
Salt to taste

Blend mustards and sugar. Add vinegar, then gradually whisk in oil. Add dill and salt. This thickens as the oil is added and sauce is allowed to stand. Refrigerate.   *Makes about 3 cups.*

CREAM CHEESE AND LEEK SOUP WITH HAM

Rich and filling, this rewarms well but should not be brought to the boiling point.

5 tablespoons butter
1 pound fresh spinach, chopped, or 2 packages (10 ounces each) frozen chopped spinach, thawed and drained
4 large leeks, chopped
6 tablespoons flour
8 cups chicken broth or bouillon

2 packages (8 ounces each) cream cheese
Salt and pepper to taste
2 cups plain yogurt
4 egg yolks
2 cups coarsely chopped cooked ham
1 cup finely chopped chives

Heat 2½ tablespoons butter in a heavy pan, add spinach and leeks, and cook until soft. Sprinkle in flour and cook for 2 minutes, stirring. Add chicken broth and cook until thickened. Simmer for 15 minutes. Mash the cream cheese in a bowl, add salt and pepper, and stir in yogurt and egg yolks. Beat until smooth. Carefully stir cheese mixture into the soup and cook over low heat for 5 minutes, stirring constantly. Sauté the ham in the remaining butter and add to soup. Serve hot, garnished with chives. *Serves 4-6.*

SUSAN'S THREE-DAY COLESLAW

*Although this keeps well, it is doubtful there will be any left
over for very long.*

1 large head of cabbage, shredded	1 green pepper, chopped or thinly sliced
1 can (7 ounces) pimiento, cut in thin strips	½ cup honey
1 medium onion, chopped or thinly sliced	1 scant cup vinegar
	2 teaspoons salt
	⅔ cup salad oil
	2 tablespoons sugar

In glass bowl toss cabbage, pimiento, onion, and green pepper
together lightly, and set aside. Mix together honey, vinegar, salt,
oil, and sugar in saucepan, and bring to a boil. Let dressing
cool, then pour over the prepared cabbage mixture. Cover, and
let age in the refrigerator for three days, stirring well each day.

Serves 10.

AVOCADO MOUSSE

A cool summer salad that looks pretty and tastes terrific.

1 package (3 ounces) lime gelatin	Juice of 1 small lemon or 1 large lime
1 cup boiling water	6 sprigs parsley, finely cut
2 cups mashed ripe avocado (3 small)	½ teaspoon salt
1 small onion, grated	¾ cup sour cream
½ cup mayonnaise	

Dissolve the gelatin in the boiling water and cool until syrupy.
Combine remaining ingredients in a blender. Whirl until
smooth — only a few seconds. Add cooled gelatin and blend
for a few seconds more. Pour into an oiled mold and

(Cont'd)

refrigerate until firm. Turn out onto a bed of lettuce, and
garnish as desired. *Serves 8.*

SCOTCH EGGS

*Easy and fun to make, these are great hot or cold. Eat whole for
brunch or lunch, or cut into wedges for hors d'oeuvres.*

½ cup soft bread
  crumbs
1 egg, beaten

1 pound best-quality
  bulk sausage
4 medium-size, hard-
  boiled eggs, peeled

Mix bread crumbs with beaten egg and sausage. Divide into 4
portions. Press each portion around an egg. (It will appear
that you have 4 small, meaty tennis balls.) Place them on a
rack in a pan and bake at 350° for about 40 minutes, until
sausage is cooked. *Serves 4.*

SCALLOPED RHUBARB

*Marvelous just as it is, but could also be made with a half cup
of strawberries added to the rhubarb.*

2 cups cut up tender
  rhubarb
1 cup sugar

3 cups fresh bread
  cubes, without
  crusts
½ cup butter, melted

Mix rhubarb and sugar in one bowl, bread cubes and melted
butter in another bowl. In a baking dish, arrange a layer of
rhubarb mixture, then a layer of bread cubes, and repeat. Bake
at 350° for 40 to 45 minutes. Serve warm, topped with
whipped cream or ice cream. *Serves 4.*

FUDGE À LA LOUISE

Everything that fudge should be — creamy, rich, and chocolatey. Makes a nice gift. In fact, Lib gave a tin of her fudge to Eleanor Roosevelt, back in the mid-1950s.

4 cups sugar	2 tablespoons butter,
3 squares dark baking	plus extra for
chocolate	greasing platters
1⅓ cups milk	1½ teaspoons vanilla
	1 cup chopped nuts

In a heavy saucepan, mix together the sugar, chocolate, and milk. Place the pan over high heat and stir constantly until the chocolate is melted and the sugar is dissolved. Bring to a full boil, and lower the heat so the candy continues to boil gently, not vigorously. Stir no more. Put a candy thermometer into the center of the mixture and cook until the temperature reaches exactly 232°. Meanwhile, grease with extra butter a large platter (turkey size) and a flat pan about 13x11 inches. When the fudge reaches 232°, pour it into the readied platter — do not scrape the pan, but let it drip out. Dot with 2 tablespoons butter and let the mixture cool until the platter feels cool underneath. Add vanilla. Take a large slotted spoon and start to stir the liquid mixture — it will take about 15 or 20 minutes. You will see a steady change from dark to light color, from glossy to dull, from liquid to solid. When the fudge begins to get dull, add the nuts and mix in thoroughly. Put fudge into the large buttered pan and press into shape with the flat of your palms. Cut into squares; store in airtight container, if there's any left. *Makes 5-6 dozen squares.*

MILE-HIGH STRAWBERRY PIE

Light and luscious. If necessary, a 10-ounce package of frozen, sweetened strawberries may be substituted for fresh, but reduce to taste the amount of sugar in the recipe.

1½ cups crushed, fresh
   strawberries
¼ cup sugar, or more
   to taste
1 tablespoon lemon
   juice

2 egg whites
½ cup heavy cream,
   whipped
9-inch pie shell or
   graham cracker
   crust, baked

Combine strawberries and sugar, and let sit for about 30 minutes. Put berries, lemon juice, and egg whites in large bowl and beat with electric mixer on medium speed until stiff peaks form. (This may take 15 minutes.) Fold in the whipped cream gently. Pile high in pie crust and freeze before serving.

Makes 1 pie.

Frieda Arkin
Essex, Massachusetts

"Man's greatest enemy is monotony," says Frieda Arkin, "and so often it's self-inflicted." Frieda brings fresh insight and imagination to her cooking, and it is evident from the delicious food she makes that she has succeeded in avoiding any hint of monotony in what can become dreary routine. She is curious and enthusiastic about the smallest detail of cooking, and this culinary curiosity has led her to a number of discoveries and innovations. For example, she found that refrigerator cookie dough slices best when it is frozen solid, and that frozen chunks of Parmesan cheese can be grated in seconds in the blender, saving time as well as knuckles. She freezes all hard cheeses and simply brings a piece to room temperature before serving.

Years ago Frieda started keeping notes on the various aspects of cooking and eventually compiled the information into a book. Today she has three books to her credit, in which she discusses kitchen tips and soup making — her own private passion.

CREAM OF LEEK AND VERMICELLI SOUP

Frieda prefers to use homemade stocks in her soups, although she will use canned broth in a pinch. "If I have a chicken or turkey carcass and don't have time to make the stock from it, I'll just break it up and freeze it, then cook the stock whenever it's convenient. Soup-making has its own philosophy."

4 leeks	¼ teaspoon ground
3 tablespoons butter	white pepper
2 tablespoons flour	2 cups milk
4 cups chicken stock	2 ounces vermicelli,
1 teaspoon salt	broken up

Wash the leeks and cut them down to 2 inches below where the green leaves separate from the whole stem. Slice the lower stems and bulbs lengthwise in half, then crosswise about ¼-inch thick. Rinse thoroughly and drain. Melt butter in a heavy soup pot and sauté the leeks gently, uncovered, for about 15 minutes. Don't let them brown. Add flour and stir well. Cook at very low heat for 10 minutes more, stirring occasionally.

Meanwhile, in a large saucepan combine chicken stock, salt, and pepper. Bring to a boil, turn down the heat, and ladle 1 cup of the stock into the leek-and-flour mixture in the soup pot. Mix well. Add 2 cups milk to the leek mixture. Cook the mixture gently, stirring often, for another 10 minutes. Turn off the heat. Bring the remaining chicken stock to a boil, add the vermicelli, and cook for about 5 minutes, until the vermicelli is soft. Add the stock and vermicelli to the soup pot, and heat through. *Serves 6-8.*

DILLED CHICK-PEA AND CHICKEN SOUP

Start out with just a couple tablespoons fresh dill or half a teaspoon of dried. Then increase the amount gradually to suit your taste.

1 tablespoon cooking oil
1 slice bacon, finely diced
1 medium onion, peeled and finely chopped
2 large stalks celery (including leaves), finely chopped
2 large carrots, peeled and finely chopped
2 level tablespoons flour
½ teaspoon ground sage

1 bay leaf
½ cup white wine
2 cups water
3 cups chicken stock
1 teaspoon Worcestershire sauce
1 can (20 ounces) chick-peas
Salt and pepper
1 cup cooked chicken, cut into thin strips
⅓ cup finely cut fresh dill, or 2 teaspoons dried (or less to taste)

Heat oil and bacon in a heavy 4-quart soup pot until bacon begins to sizzle. Add onion, celery, and carrots and cook, covered, until the vegetables are softened (about 15 minutes). Add flour, sage, bay leaf, wine, and ½ cup of the water; mix well and bring to a simmer, uncovered. Cook for 10 minutes, stirring often. Remove the bay leaf. Add chicken stock, remaining water, and Worcestershire sauce, and mix well. Puree chick-peas in a blender and add to the soup. Bring to a full boil. Add salt and pepper to taste. Add cooked chicken and dill, and heat through. *Serves 6-8.*

PARSNIP SOUP

Absolutely delicious. Be sure to include the Parmesan cheese, which adds a special touch of its own.

4 tablespoons butter	1 teaspoon salt
1 pound parsnips,	2 cups water
peeled and cut up	Black pepper
1 cup chopped celery	⅓ cup chopped fresh
(including leaves)	parsley, or 2
3 cups chicken stock	teaspoons dried
3 tablespoons flour	Parmesan cheese,
1 cup cold water	freshly grated
¼ teaspoon grated	
nutmeg	

Melt butter in heavy soup pot and sauté parsnips and celery, stirring with a wooden spoon until the vegetables are coated with butter. Cover and cook over medium heat for 10 minutes, stirring occasionally. Meanwhile, heat the chicken stock in a saucepan, and after 10 minutes add to the soup pot. Stir well and put 1 cup of the soup (including plenty of solids) into a blender or food processor along with the flour, 1 cup cold water, nutmeg, and salt. Blend at high speed, and return to the soup pot. Add 2 cups water and heat to a good simmer for 5 minutes. Season to taste with pepper. Return another cup of soup to the blender and add parsley. Blend well and return the puree to the soup pot. Heat to a simmer. Just before serving, sprinkle with freshly grated Parmesan cheese.

Serves 6-8.

CURRY FREEZER COOKIES

There's a definite "bite" to these crispy cookies, which are a lovely golden yellow and better suited for a seasoned palate than for children.

1 cup butter	½ teaspoon baking soda
2 cups brown sugar	1 teaspoon baking
2 teaspoons vanilla	powder
2 eggs, beaten	½ teaspoon salt
1½ cups broken	2 teaspoons curry
walnuts	powder
3 cups flour	

Cream butter and brown sugar; add vanilla and eggs, then walnuts. Add sifted dry ingredients and mix well. Form into 2 to 4 rolls, wrap in waxed paper, and freeze. While still frozen, cut into thin slices and bake on ungreased cookie sheets at 350° for about 12 minutes. Let cool for about 5 minutes, then remove and cool on newspaper covered with paper toweling.

Makes about 4 dozen.

CHARLES BALLOU
Brookfield, Vermont

While working as cook for the residents of the Tranquility Nursing Home in Randolph, Vermont, Charlie Ballou discovered he had a flair for cooking contests. Twice he entered recipes in national contests and twice he won prizes. Then he submitted a recipe to the Professional Pineapple Cooking Contest sponsored by the Pineapple Growers Association of Hawaii, and from over 3,000 entries, his Pineapple Rise (a pineapple gelatin soufflé) was a finalist in the dessert category.

Charlie and his wife, Sherry, were flown to Hawaii for a week — all expenses paid — where he and the thirty-five other finalists prepared their specialties before a panel of judges. Although Charlie's dessert didn't win the grand prize ($20,000), the experience didn't dampen his enthusiasm for cooking or for homesteading. He and Sherry continue to raise all the vegetables they need for their family of four on their twelve-acre farm in the White River valley. "If you're going to take the time to eat," says Charlie, "you might as well eat the best," and it is a point of pride with the Ballous that eating the best naturally means the produce from their valley.

CHARLIE'S GRAHAM BREAD

"This is almost like Boston Brown Bread. It's our favorite Saturday night meal with baked beans."

2 teaspoons baking
  soda
2 tablespoons vinegar
2 cups milk
2 cups graham flour
1 cup soy flour
½ teaspoon (sea) salt

1 cup raisins
½ cup chopped nuts
  (preferably walnuts)
¾ cup molasses
½ tablespoon melted
  shortening or oil

Mix the baking soda and the vinegar separately into the milk. Combine dry ingredients, including the raisins and nuts, and add molasses and shortening. Add the milk mixture to the dry ingredients. Stir until well blended. Pour into 2 well-greased, medium-size loaf pans. Bake at 350° for 45 minutes or until done. Remove from pans and let cool on rack. *Makes 2 loaves.*

VEGETABLE QUICHE

Charlie created this recipe at home with Sherry and tried it on his friends at the nursing home. It turned out to be one of his prize winners.

9-inch pie shell,
  unbaked
2 cups cooked
  vegetables
4 eggs, beaten

¾ cup milk
⅛ teaspoon each,
  nutmeg and pepper
1½ cups grated
  cheddar cheese

Pour your favorite drained vegetable (or mixture of vegetables) into the unbaked pie shell. Beat eggs, milk, and spices together and pour over vegetables. Sprinkle grated cheese evenly over the top. Bake at 325° for 45 to 60 minutes, or until knife inserted comes out clean. Cut and serve. *Serves 4-6.*

ZUCCHINI-POTATO FRITTATA

Serve this as a light lunch or summer supper, accompanied by a green salad, homemade bread, and white wine.

1 cup raw zucchini,
  peeled and coarsely
  grated
½ teaspoon (sea) salt
2 eggs, separated
2 medium potatoes,
  cooked, peeled, and
  mashed

½ onion, chopped and
  sautéed
2 ounces Parmesan
  cheese, freshly grated
Dash of garlic powder
Salt and pepper to taste

Sprinkle zucchini with (sea) salt and let stand for 10 minutes. Drain. Combine zucchini with lightly beaten egg yolks. Add mashed potato, sautéed onion, half the grated cheese, the garlic powder, and salt and pepper. Beat egg whites with pinch of salt until stiff. Fold into zucchini mixture. Pour into small casserole. Sprinkle remaining cheese on top. Bake at 350° for 30 to 40 minutes, or until brown. Serve hot. *Serves 3-4.*

APPLESAUCE PUDDING

Another recipe-contest winner for Charlie. For best results, use a spicy and strong-flavored applesauce so the crumb mixture doesn't overpower the apple flavor.

4 cups crumbs (cookie, cracker, or dried bread crumbs)	1½ teaspoons cinnamon
¼ cup honey	1 tablespoon oil
	4 cups seasoned applesauce

Blend crumbs (which may include wheat germ or sesame seeds to total 4 cups), honey, cinnamon, and oil. Put ⅓ of the mixture into a greased oblong glass baking dish. Put half of the applesauce on top of the crumbs. Repeat crumb layer and applesauce layer. Top with last third of crumb mixture. Chill and serve. *Makes 6-8 servings.*

PINEAPPLE RISE

Especially appealing in the summer. When Charlie competed in the Professional Pineapple Cooking Contest in Hawaii, he discovered that cooking technique and style counted in the judging as much as the creation itself.

1 can (20 ounces) crushed pineapple	⅛ teaspoon salt
1½ cups sugar, or ½ cup honey	1½ cups heavy cream, whipped
¾ ounce plain gelatin	Whipped cream and strawberries for garnish
6 egg yolks	
6 egg whites	

Drain and grind or puree pineapple. Add half the sugar or honey. Remove 1 cup of puree and sprinkle gelatin over the top

(Cont'd)

of it to soften. Combine egg yolks and rest of sugar or honey and cook over low heat or in double boiler, stirring until mixture thickens. Add the gelatin mixture and stir until the gelatin dissolves. Cool to lukewarm and add remaining puree. Whip egg whites and salt in a bowl until foamy. Fold in whipped cream. Gently fold in pineapple mixture. Pour into mold or oblong pan. Chill until firm, approximately 2 hours. Garnish with whipped cream and strawberries.   *Serves 10-12.*

BETTY BALSLEY
Wellfleet, Massachusetts

Betty Balsley of Wellfleet, Massachusetts, keeps a tide chart on the little kitchen table where she and her husband, Frank, eat breakfast and plan the day's activities. On Wednesdays and Sundays, when clamming is permitted in Wellfleet Bay, the run of daily life is adjusted to the tides. She and Frank go clamming and fishing several times a week in good weather to get the raw materials for some of her famous seafood specialties.

"Clams and oysters will keep up to a week," Betty says. "Sometimes if I have a lot on hand, I'll shuck them and freeze them, which works quite well, although they're never quite as good as when they're fresh. They say people on the Cape used to pack clams and oysters in seaweed and put them in the barn for the whole winter. I've heard about that — but we've never tried it!"

FRIED OYSTERS

Fried oysters can be tricky to make, because they so easily over-cook and toughen, but Betty's are delicate and golden brown, and her secret is frying them in olive oil. Also, after rinsing the oysters, she returns them to their liquid for a while to "get them back into their own environment."

2 dozen fresh oysters	Lemon wedges
½ cup olive oil	Mayonnaise or tartar
1 cup flour	sauce
Black pepper to taste	

Shuck oysters, saving all juice. Rinse oysters to get out any pieces of shell. Strain juice and return oysters to juice until ready to fry. Cover bottom of skillet with about ¼ inch of olive oil and heat to very hot. Gently pat oysters dry between paper towels and shake in paper bag with flour and pepper to taste. Fry in hot olive oil until golden. Drain on brown paper and serve hot with lemon wedges and mayonnaise or tartar sauce.

Serves 6.

STUFFED CLAMS

When preparing clams, Betty removes the dark stomachs: "They wouldn't hurt the recipe, but I remove them for aesthetic reasons." She bakes the mixture in littleneck clam shells and frequently makes a double batch so she can freeze half to keep on hand for unexpected company. "You can use canned clams in this recipe if you don't have access to fresh ones."

1 cup chopped littleneck (quahog) clams and liquid
½ cup finely chopped onion
½ cup finely chopped celery
¼ cup finely chopped green pepper
4 tablespoons butter
2 tablespoons flour
1 tablespoon grated Parmesan cheese
¼ teaspoon salt
Dash of black pepper
Dash of Worcestershire sauce
12 Ritz crackers, crushed
1 tablespoon butter, melted
Paprika

Remove stomachs from clams and grind clams in a food mill or chop them by hand until you have 1 cup of clams and liquid. Cook onion, celery, and green pepper in 4 tablespoons butter until vegetables are tender, but not brown. Stir in flour, cheese, and seasonings. Add ¼ cup of crushed crackers, and mix well. Stir in clams with their liquid, and cook and stir until mixture is thick and bubbly. Divide mixture among 15 to 18 littleneck clam shells, or 10 to 12 larger clam shells, or spoon into a casserole dish (as a last resort). Combine remaining crumbs and 1 tablespoon melted butter and sprinkle over filled shells. Sprinkle lightly with paprika. Bake at 350° for 10 to 15 minutes. Serve hot. *Serves 6-8.*

BAKED BLUEFISH

Baked fish fillets drizzled with garlic-and-dill-flavored butter.
Garnish with thin slices of lemon and sprigs of fresh parsley.

Bluefish fillets	Butter
Vinegar	Garlic clove, crushed
Garlic powder	Dill seed to taste
Black pepper	Lemon

Place fish fillets in foil-lined pan, skin side down. Sprinkle
lightly with vinegar, garlic powder, and pepper, and dot with
butter. Bake uncovered at 350° for 20 to 30 minutes,
depending upon the thickness of the fish. Melt half a stick of
butter (or more, depending on amount of fish being served)
and add crushed garlic and dill seed. Serve hot over fish with
lemon.   *Serving quantity depends on size*
and number of fillets used.

HADDOCK CASSEROLE

"My mother's haddock casserole — it's a simple, simple dish,
but delicious." When haddock isn't available, Betty substitutes
scrod or any other good white fish, which she poaches quickly by
covering with water and bringing to a boil. Then she covers the
pan, turns off the heat, and lets the fish cook in the hot water
until flaky.

1 pound fresh or frozen haddock	½ cup milk
3 tablespoons butter or margarine	¼ cup poaching liquid
2 to 3 tablespoons flour	½ pound cheddar cheese, cut in small chunks or grated
	Dash of pepper

(Cont'd)

Poach fish in a large pan until flaky; reserve a little of the water. Melt butter, stir in flour, and gradually stir in mixture of milk and poaching water to make a thick white sauce. Add the cheese to the sauce and heat until the cheese is melted. In a greased casserole, alternate layers of fish and cheese sauce, ending with sauce. Bake uncovered at 350° for 30 to 45 minutes. Serve hot, accompanied by sweet potatoes. *Serves 2-3.*

BEST-EVER BLUEBERRY MUFFINS

Betty has life-long ties with the Wellfleet area, where she spent many childhood summers. "When I was a girl, my Aunt Alice and I would go blueberrying here, pick beach plums, or bake bread. She and my mother taught me to cook."

1¾ cups sifted flour	1 egg, well beaten
4 tablespoons sugar	¾ to 1 cup milk
2½ teaspoons baking powder	⅓ cup oil
¾ teaspoon salt	1 cup fresh wild blueberries

Sift together flour, 2 tablespoons sugar, baking powder, and salt. Make a well in the center. Combine egg, milk, and oil, and pour into well in the dry ingredients, stirring quickly just to moisten. Do not stir too much! Toss blueberries with remaining 2 tablespoons sugar and gently stir into batter. Fill greased muffin tins two-thirds full. Sprinkle tops with sugar. Bake for 20 to 25 minutes at 400°.   *Makes 1 dozen.*

AUNT ALICE'S COFFEE CLOUD
SPONGE CAKE

A recipe with childhood associations for Betty, this cake was always served with lemonade after the Fourth of July fireworks. As the name implies, it is light in texture, with a mild coffee flavor enhanced by the satiny icing.

1 tablespoon instant coffee	½ teaspoon cream of tartar
1 cup boiling water	2 cups sugar
2 cups sifted all-purpose flour	1 teaspoon vanilla
3 teaspoons baking powder	1 cup finely ground pecans or walnuts
½ teaspoon salt	Coffee Icing (recipe follows)
6 eggs, separated	

Dissolve instant coffee in boiling water, and cool. Sift together flour, baking powder, and salt. Beat egg whites with cream of tartar in a large bowl until soft mounds form. Add ½ cup of the sugar to the egg whites a little at a time, and continue beating until very stiff. Do not underbeat. Set whites aside. Beat the egg yolks in a large mixing bowl until blended, and gradually add remaining 1½ cups sugar and 1 teaspoon vanilla. Beat at high speed until thick and lemon-colored (about 5 minutes). Add the dry ingredients alternately with the cooled coffee to the egg yolk mixture, beginning and ending with dry ingredients. Blend thoroughly. Fold in nuts. Lightly fold in the beaten egg whites until evenly blended. Pour into an ungreased 10-inch tube pan and bake at 350° for 60 to 70 minutes. Remove from oven and invert immediately onto platter. Let pan stay in place at least 1 hour before removing. Frost with Coffee Icing. *Serves 16.*

(Cont'd)

COFFEE ICING

2 tablespoons butter
2 cups sifted
   confectioners sugar
1½ teaspoons instant
   coffee

2 to 3 tablespoons milk
Chopped nuts
   (optional)

Cream butter. Blend in confectioners sugar and instant coffee and mix well. Gradually add milk until icing is of spreading consistency. Frost cake and sprinkle with chopped nuts if desired.

MARY BOSQUI
Westport, Connecticut

Mary Bosqui loves to surround herself with family and valued friends, and meals are an integral part of those gatherings. Whether the group is large or small, Mary's table is always set with wholesome, tasty, and artfully prepared dishes. "Most of my recipes come from family and friends. I always come back to my old favorites — they're uncomplicated, made from ingredients I usually have on hand, and I enjoy thinking about the people when I make their recipes."

When cooking for a large number of guests, Mary tries to prepare as much as possible ahead of time ("That makes entertaining pleasant, even for the hostess!"), and she includes at least one main dish that can be made in advance, then reheated and kept warm in a chafing dish. She uses her pressure cooker for last-minute vegetables.

Mary is a firm believer in accompanying a meal with pickles, chutney, or relishes. "You can serve a full meal — meat, potatoes, vegetables, dessert — but it's not a dinner without pickles or chutney." Consequently, she has to keep her kitchen shelves well stocked with these homemade condiments, all of which, needless to say, are consumed with relish!

CHICKEN À LA KING

Green pepper and pimiento make this old favorite look very festive and add a little extra zip! Delicious as an everyday meal on toast or dressed up for company with patty shells.

3 to 4 tablespoons
  butter or margarine
1 cup sliced
  mushrooms
2 tablespoons chopped
  green pepper
6 tablespoons flour
½ teaspoon salt
½ teaspoon celery salt
Dash of cayenne pepper

¾ cup milk
¾ cup light cream
1 cup chicken stock
2 cups diced cooked
  chicken
1 tablespoon chopped
  parsley
1 tablespoon finely cut
  pimiento

Melt butter. Add mushrooms and green pepper, and sauté for 5 minutes on low heat, stirring occasionally. Mix flour and seasonings together, and add gradually to butter to make a roux, stirring constantly. Add milk, cream, and chicken stock slowly, continuing to stir until sauce thickens. Add chicken, parsley, and pimiento. Adjust seasonings to taste. Increase flour or cream to achieve desired thickness. *Serves 4.*

OLIVE'S HOBO BREAD

A rich brown bread laced with raisins and baked in one-pound coffee tins. It is an eggless quick bread that gets its moisture from the oil and raisin liquid, and keeps well for days.

4 teaspoons baking
  soda
2 cups boiling water
2 cups dark raisins

4 cups flour
2 cups sugar
½ teaspoon salt
4 tablespoons oil

(Cont'd)

Mix baking soda and water together and pour over the raisins. Let stand overnight without stirring. Next morning sift together the flour, sugar, and salt, and stir this into the raisin mixture with a spoon. Add oil and continue to mix well with a spoon. Batter will be thick. Grease and flour three 1-pound coffee cans and put one third of the batter into each can, leaving top of can open for baking. (Cans will be about half full.) Bake at 350° for half an hour; reduce heat to 325° and bake another half hour. Near the end of the baking, cover the open cans with foil if necessary to prevent excessive browning. Test breads with a long cake tester and remove from oven. Lay cans on their sides and turn occasionally to loosen the bread. (Be sure to do this.) Remove from cans when cooled. *Makes 3 loaves.*

LUCIA'S PEACH CHUTNEY

Using this recipe from her younger daughter, Mary usually makes a year's supply at a time. She serves it at buffets to enhance cold sliced ham or beef.

4 cups peeled, pitted, and cut up peaches
2 cups cider vinegar
3 cups sugar
½ pound seedless raisins
Small jar of candied ginger, cut fine; or 2 tablespoons minced fresh ginger root
1 tablespoon mustard seed
Handful of chopped onion
2 garlic cloves, pressed (optional)

Place peaches in large saucepan. Combine vinegar and sugar and bring to a boil. Pour over peaches and add raisins, ginger, mustard seed, onion, and garlic. Cook for 2 hours, stirring occasionally to prevent sticking. Pour into sterile jars and seal, using boiling-water bath if desired. *Makes about 5 pints.*

AUNT MYLA'S GREEN TOMATO PICKLE

When making her pickles and relishes, Mary always tries to use the freshest produce she can find — some of which comes from her own backyard garden.

4 quarts sliced green tomatoes
20 onions, sliced thin
1 cup table salt
4 quarts thinly sliced green cabbage
6 cups cider vinegar
8 cups sugar

2 tablespoons mustard seed
4 tablespoons celery seed
4 green and 4 red peppers, finely chopped
2 tablespoons turmeric (optional)

Place tomatoes and onions in separate bowls and pour ½ cup salt over each bowl. Let stand overnight. In the morning drain the tomatoes, rinse the onions, and combine. Add cabbage. Combine vinegar and sugar and boil for two minutes. Add mustard seed, celery seed, green and red peppers, and turmeric if desired. Bring to a boil and pour over tomato mixture. Pour hot into sterilized jars and process in boiling-water bath if desired. *Makes 12 pints.*

CAROLYN'S WATERMELON PICKLE

This recipe, from Mary's elder daughter, provides the occasion for an annual summer watermelon party. These crunchy, translucent, sweet-sour chunks are positively addictive, and make a piquant addition to a simple meal. They go so fast that you might want to double the recipe.

Rind from half of a large watermelon
Cold water
3 pounds sugar
1 pint cider vinegar

½ ounce whole cloves
½ ounce whole allspice
1 cinnamon stick, broken

(Cont'd)

Slice watermelon rind into 1-inch strips and peel off the green skin. Cut the rind into 1-inch chunks. Cover with cold water and boil for 20 minutes. Drain. Blend sugar and cider vinegar. In a small square of cheesecloth place the cloves, allspice, and cinnamon, and tie the cloth firmly to make a bag. Add to the sugar and vinegar. Bring the sugar and vinegar to a boil and pour over the watermelon rind. Cover and allow to stand overnight. The next day drain off and save the syrup and spices and bring them to a boil again; pour over the rind and let stand overnight a second time. On the third day boil the rind and syrup together until the rind is transparent and the syrup is the consistency of honey. Place rind in sterilized jars, cover completely with syrup, and seal; process in boiling-water bath if desired.   *Makes 4-5 pints.*

MOTHER'S FORGOTTEN COOKIES

These meringue-like cookies are placed in a preheated oven, which is immediately turned off, and they bake overnight as the oven cools down. An easy and fun way to concoct a batch of sweets — ideal in the summer, and fancy enough for Christmas.

2 egg whites, at room
  temperature
¾ cup sugar
1 package (6 ounces)
  chocolate chips

A drop or two of green
  food coloring
  (optional)
4 drops mint extract
  (about ¼ teaspoon)

Preheat oven to 375°. Beat egg whites until stiff, adding sugar gradually. Fold in chocolate chips, coloring, and mint extract. Drop by teaspoonfuls on an ungreased cookie sheet, using an upward twist of the spoon to form peaks. Place in preheated oven and turn oven off immediately. Leave in oven with door closed overnight — and enjoy the cookies the next morning!
                        Makes about 30 large or 45 small cookies.

61

IRENE'S TROPICAL CARROT CAKE

Carrot cake par excellence. Crushed pineapple makes this a moist cake, complemented by a lemon-flavored cream cheese frosting.

2 cups flour	2 cups finely shredded
2 teaspoons baking	carrots (about 6
powder	medium size)
1 teaspoon baking soda	1 can (8 ounces)
1 teaspoon cinnamon	crushed pineapple,
½ teaspoon nutmeg	with liquid pressed
½ teaspoon allspice	out *thoroughly*
½ teaspoon salt	1 cup chopped walnuts
4 eggs	Cream Cheese Frosting
2 cups sugar	(recipe follows)
1¼ cups oil	

Sift dry ingredients together and set aside. Beat eggs lightly in a large mixing bowl. Gradually beat in sugar until the mixture is thick and lemon-colored. With a rubber spatula, gradually stir in the oil. Add dry ingedients, shredded carrots, pineapple, and walnuts and stir until well mixed. Turn into a greased and floured 13x9-inch pan. Bake at 350° for 55 to 60 minutes, or until done. Cool on rack, and frost when thoroughly cool with Cream Cheese Frosting. *Serves 10-12.*

CREAM CHEESE FROSTING

4 ounces cream cheese,	1 tablespoon lemon
at room temperature	juice, strained
¼ cup butter or	2½ cups sifted
margarine, at room	confectioners sugar
temperature	

Combine all ingredients, and beat until fluffy. Spread onto cooled cake.

DOTTIE'S COCONUT-LEMON BARS

Very rich and tangy — delicious with or without raisins and walnuts. A special treat to pack in a lunch or enjoy as an afternoon snack.

2 cups flour
½ cup butter or
   margarine
¼ cup brown sugar,
   packed
3 eggs, well beaten
2 cups brown sugar,
   packed
½ teaspoon salt

1 cup finely shredded
   coconut
½ cup seedless raisins
½ cup chopped
   walnuts
2 tablespoons lemon
   juice
1 teaspoon grated
   lemon rind

Mix together flour, butter, and ¼ cup brown sugar. Press firmly into the bottom of a lightly greased 13x9-inch pan. Bake for 10 minutes at 350°. Cool. Mix together the eggs, 2 cups brown sugar, and salt. Stir in coconut, raisins, walnuts, lemon juice and rind. Spread evenly over the partially baked bottom layer. Bake for about 20 minutes at 350°. Top will be lightly browned. When cool, cut into bars. If desired, sprinkle with confectioners sugar before serving. *Makes about 24 bars.*

MARGUERITE (DIMINO) BUONOPANE
The North End, Boston, Massachusetts

"There are some things you know you can do well," says Marguerite Buonopane, "and ravioli is one of mine." She does it so well, in fact, that her ravioli is a culinary celebrity in Boston's Italian North End.

Because ravioli is time-consuming to make, Marguerite likes to prepare it in large batches and serve it on festive occasions. It is really "more tedious than difficult," she says.

There are three steps to successful ravioli making: the dough, the filling, and the sauce. The big secret with dough, she says, is maintaining a positive attitude: "Don't be afraid of it. If it's mushy, throw in more flour." Marguerite suggests making the filling for ravioli the night before, to give the flavors a chance to mix. And then there's the sauce — what she calls gravy. "There's no need for the gravy to cook for hours. Our mothers did it only because they had to be home all day. They would put the pot of gravy on the oil stove, and would come by and stir it all day long. But nobody wants to do that today."

Never overlook the conveniences found in a local supermarket for making a full-bodied sauce, she advises. "I buy Pastene 'kitchen-ready' tomatoes. I wouldn't use anything else. The tomatoes are already ground and peeled. I won't use canned Italian tomatoes because they're filled with water. I want the body of the tomato."

For a number of years Marguerite has been teaching a course in Italian cooking. It meets for eight weeks and is held either at her home in the heart of the North End, or at the

North End Union. Her class, which often includes men, attracts many young people of Italian descent who feel they have lost the Old World ways in their homes. With Marguerite's instruction, however, they are rediscovering the art of Italian cooking, and keeping it alive for their family and friends to enjoy.

STUFFED ARTICHOKES

It upsets Marguerite that so many people "shy away from cooking food they are unfamiliar with. If I can give them confidence to try anything, then I've succeeded."

6 medium artichokes	Salt and pepper to
Oil	taste
1½ cups grated soft	1 garlic clove, finely
Italian bread	chopped
¼ cup chopped fresh	1¼ cups water
parsley	1 teaspoon salt
½ cup grated Romano	3 garlic cloves, crushed
cheese	Oil

Soak artichokes in cold water for about half an hour to release dirt. Place on countertop and trim points off leaves with scissors; cut off bottoms so they will sit flat. Stand artichokes upside down, and give them a firm whack so that the leaves open slightly.

Mix enough oil with bread to moisten. Add parsley, cheese, salt and pepper, and garlic, and mix well. Fill insides of leaves with mixture. Place stuffed artichokes in pan of water to which 1 teaspoon salt and 3 garlic cloves have been added. Sprinkle more oil on top of artichokes and simmer *slowly* for 45 minutes. *Serves 6.*

CHICKEN CACCIATORE

Green peas give this familiar favorite a unique twist.

1 chicken, cut in small pieces
Oil to cover bottom of pan
1 large onion, chopped
1 large garlic clove, chopped
Salt and pepper to taste
Pinch of red pepper flakes
1 tablespoon tomato paste

1 medium-size can crushed tomatoes
1 large can peas
2 to 3 green peppers, thickly sliced
½ to ¾ pound mushrooms (if small, don't cut; if large, cut in large chunks)
Parsley to taste

Fry chicken in heavy skillet in oil. When all pieces are golden brown, add onion, garlic, salt and pepper, and red pepper flakes. Sauté until slightly browned. Add tomato paste and mix well. Add tomatoes and turn chicken until all pieces are well coated. Add *juice* only from can of peas. Lightly salt and pepper again. Sauté for 25 minutes. Add green peppers and mushrooms, and sauté for 10 minutes. Add can of peas. *Do not mix or cook anymore.* Turn off stove and let sit for 5 minutes. Sprinkle with chopped fresh parsley.   *Serves 5.*

LOBSTER FRA DIABLO

Clams, shrimp, and lobster — a seafood lover's dream-come-true.

1 whole onion,
  chopped
1 cup sliced fresh
  mushrooms
1 tablespoon chopped
  fresh parsley
Pinch of red pepper
  flakes
Pinch of oregano
3 bay leaves
Few drops Tabasco
  sauce (optional)

Enough oil to coat
  bottom of pan
1 cup chicken bouillon
2 to 5 lobsters
¼ to ½ cup sherry
Salt to taste
½ dozen clams in shell
½ to 1 pound shrimp in
  shells

Sauté first 7 ingredients in oil until onions are transparent. Add
chicken bouillon and lobsters. Sprinkle with sherry and salt,
then cover to steam for about 20 minutes. Add clams and
shrimp in shells for last 15 minutes. (Leaving them in shells
keeps juices in.) Simmer, covered, until shells open. *Serves 2-5.*

LENTIL SOUP

A hearty, versatile soup that lends itself to countless variations.

½ pound lentils,
  picked over and
  rinsed
1½ quarts water
2 to 3 stalks celery and
  leaves, finely chopped
2 small carrots, finely
  chopped
Chopped parsley (a
  sprinkle)
1 onion, chopped

1 garlic clove, chopped
Salt and pepper to
  taste
1 tablespoon oil
3 ripe tomatoes, or ½
  cup canned
Bay leaf
1 pound small shells,
  or 1 pound elbow or
  ditalini macaroni

(Cont'd)

Cook all but last ingredient in heavy saucepan until mixture comes to a boil. Let simmer for half an hour or longer, adding more water if needed. (Oil in recipe accelerates cooking time.) Cook pasta according to package directions, drain, add to lentil soup, and cook for 5 minutes more.   *Serves 6.*

RAVIOLI

A lot of work, but a great finished product. Actually fun to make if you allow yourself plenty of time. Or do what Marguerite suggests — invite your friends to a ravioli-making party. Have them bring their own rolling pins, and make enough for everyone to take some home.

Dough:

2½ pounds (about 10 cups) unbleached, unsifted flour (Marguerite prefers King Arthur)	1 tablespoon salt 3 medium eggs Boiling water as needed

Make a well in the flour on a pastry board. Add salt. Partially beat eggs before adding to flour. Add eggs gradually; mix with fingers until dough resembles the texture of cornmeal. Sprinkle the boiling water on mixture starting with only ¼ cup, and work well into dough. Add more boiling water as needed until dough is smooth and pliable, but not too soft. Knead dough for about 5 minutes. Pat with some water, cover, and let sit for about half an hour. Prepare filling and meat sauce while waiting for the dough.

(Cont'd)

Filling:

2 pounds ricotta cheese	1 small garlic clove, pressed
5 medium eggs	8 parsley sprigs, finely chopped
Salt and pepper to taste	
1 cup grated Parmesan or Romano cheese	

Blend all ingredients together. Let sit overnight, if possible, to allow flavors to mix.

Meat Sauce:

Oil	1 can (6 ounces) tomato paste
1 garlic clove, chopped	
1 small onion, chopped	1 can (28 ounces) ground, peeled tomatoes (Pastene kitchen-ready)
Dash of sweet basil, red pepper flakes, and oregano	
½ pound lean ground beef	Bay leaf
	1 can water (using 28-ounce tomato can)
½ pound ground pork (beef may be substituted)	

Put enough oil in pan to coat bottom. Sauté garlic, onion, and seasonings over medium heat until onion is lightly golden. Add all the meat. Cook until slightly browned. Blend tomato paste in well; stir a few minutes. Add tomatoes and bay leaf and stir. Pour in water. Reduce heat and allow sauce to simmer for up to 1 hour, stirring frequently. (Remove bay leaf before serving.)

(Cont'd)

To Assemble:

Divide dough into fourths and roll out only one fourth at a time, keeping the rest covered. Roll dough as thin as possible. Place heaping teaspoon of filling 1½ inches from edge of dough and continue to place filling in straight row across the dough, being careful to leave 1½ inches between each spoonful. Fold over the edge of the dough to completely cover the first row of filling. With your fingers, gently press down on dough around the mounds of filling. Using a 2½-inch ravioli cutter, cut around the mounds. A pastry cutter or small glass may be used instead — but be sure to seal the edges with a fork. Continue in this manner until all the dough is used. (The dough that you don't want to use may be frozen in a plastic bag and used at a later date to make more ravioli or even pasta. It may also be kept in the refrigerator up to 5 days.)

To Freeze:

This recipe may very well make much more than you will want to serve at one time. The ravioli can be frozen *before* it is cooked. Sprinkle flour or cornmeal on cookie sheets and place ravioli in a single layer on the sheets and freeze. After the ravioli is frozen, which takes about 20 minutes, it may be placed in plastic bags. This way the pieces won't stick to one another.

To Cook:

Bring 6 to 8 quarts of salted water to a boil. Gradually add the ravioli and cook until tender, about 15 to 20 minutes. It is best not to overcrowd the pot, because you will need to

(Cont'd)

continually press the ravioli to the bottom of the pot so that they will cook evenly.

To Serve:

Carefully remove ravioli and let them drain well. Place them in a serving dish and cover with meat sauce and a layer of grated Parmesan or Romano cheese. Continue in this manner until you have used all the cooked ravioli. Serve with a tossed salad, garlic bread, and wine. Enjoy your meal and all the compliments you will receive!   *Enough sauce to serve 6, ravioli to serve 9.*

BISCOTTI (Italian Cookies)

Attractive, crunchy, semicircular-shaped cookies, with a mild anise flavor and slightly nutty taste.

2 cups sifted flour	½ cup margarine,
2 teaspoons baking	melted
powder	2 teaspoons vanilla
½ teaspoon salt	1 tablespoon anise
3 eggs, well beaten	extract
1 cup sugar	1 cup chopped walnuts

Sift together flour, baking powder, and salt. In separate bowl combine remaining ingredients, mixing well. Add flour mixture to other ingredients and beat until smooth and satiny. If too soft, work in more flour. Roll into little loaves (3x1-inch). Place on greased cookie sheet. Bake at 350° until brown, about 15 to 20 minutes. When cool, slice into ½-inch slices. Arrange slices on baking sheet, and return to oven to dry out (about 10 minutes longer). Cool thoroughly and store in covered container.   *Makes 6 dozen.*

ITALIAN TWISTS

Crispy and light, with a handsome shape. Serve as an accompaniment to ice cream, pudding, or chocolate mousse.

½ teaspoon salt	1 teaspoon vanilla
4 egg yolks	1 teaspoon rum
1 egg white	1 to 1½ cups flour
¼ cup confectioners sugar	Crisco shortening
	Confectioners sugar

Add salt to eggs and beat 10 minutes. Add sugar and flavorings and beat until well blended. Fold in flour a little at a time until dough can be kneaded. Transfer to a well-floured board and knead until the dough blisters. Cut in halves. Roll very thin, and cut into strips about 4 inches long. Slit each piece in center, and pull one end through slit. Make sure knot is in center. Fry in hot shortening until lightly browned. Drain on paper towel. Sprinkle with confectioners sugar.

Makes 4 dozen.

ANN CHANDLER
Amherst, New Hampshire

"People have a lot of misconceptions about Mexican food," says Ann Chandler. "They picture it as a steady round of tacos, tostados, enchiladas, and chalupas. A Mexican family would never serve all those things at one meal. They might have roast chicken and *sopa de arroz* [a rice dish], with freshly made flour tortillas instead of biscuits. Or pork chops with *frijoles refritos*, what we call refried beans, although that's a mistranslation — it really just means cooked pinto beans that are mashed and reheated. And Mexicans do like spicy food, but the chilies and *salsa picante* [a spicy-hot sauce] are served separately, and considered to be condiments."

One of the attractive features of Mexican cooking is that most dishes can either be partly prepared ahead or made fairly quickly at mealtime. In addition, Mexican cooking is individualistic: use as much or as little hot sauce as desired, or add an extra topping to a tostado, and everything will still turn out fine. And it *is* possible to make good Mexican food using what is found on New England grocery shelves. "As long as you can get pinto beans and tortillas, you're set," Ann says.

SALSA PICANTE (Hot Sauce)

This sauce goes with just about any kind of Mexican food and can be made as spicy or as mild as you wish. For a smoother consistency, mix it in a blender for just a few seconds.

3 tomatoes, chopped
1 tablespoon minced onion
1 jalapeño pepper, minced (remove seeds)

1 small garlic clove, minced
½ teaspoon vinegar
Dash of cumin or cilantro (optional)

Mix all ingredients together. Will keep for several days in the refrigerator. *Makes about 2 cups.*

FRIJOLES (Mexican Beans)

Serve these beans with Salsa Picante (preceding recipe) on the side, or mix in chopped jalapeño or green chilies if a hotter flavor is desired.

1 pound dried pinto beans
1 cup coarsely chopped onion
1 to 2 garlic cloves, crushed

2-inch square salt pork
5 cups water
1 teaspoon salt
¼ to ½ teaspoon black pepper

Pick over beans and wash them. Place in a heavy saucepan and add all but last 2 ingredients. Cover, bring to a full boil, turn heat off, and let stand for 2 hours. Return to a boil, then reduce heat to a simmer. Cook for 1 hour, or until tender. Season with salt and pepper and discard salt pork before serving. *Serves 8.*

(Cont'd)

Frijoles Refritos: Mash 2 cups of cooked and seasoned beans, and fry in 3 tablespoons butter or bacon drippings. Turn onto a heated platter, sprinkle with grated Monterey Jack cheese, and serve with Salsa Picante.

Burritos: Spread some Frijoles Refritos on heated flour tortillas. Sprinkle with minced onion or grated cheese or bits of cooked meat, roll up, and eat.

SOPA DE ARROZ

This literally means "soup of rice"; however, in this soup the liquid is totally absorbed by the ingredients. The dish is also called Mexican Rice.

1 cup uncooked rice (do not use minute or converted rice)
3 tablespoons oil or bacon drippings
1 onion, sliced
1 green pepper, sliced
1 tomato, peeled and sliced

2 cups liquid: boiling water, chicken broth, beef broth, or a combination of 1 cup tomato sauce and 1 cup liquid of your choice
½ teaspoon salt
¼ teaspoon pepper

Lightly brown the rice in hot oil in a large saucepan, stirring constantly. Arrange onion, green pepper, and tomato on top of the rice. Add the liquid, salt, and pepper, and reduce heat to a simmer. Cook covered for 15 to 20 minutes, or until rice has absorbed the liquid and is tender. For a variation, add pieces of cooked meat, garbanzo beans, or peas. Allow guests to add Salsa Picante to suit themselves. *Serves 4-6.*

CHILAQUILLES

Excellent served with barbecued chicken. For a spicier dish, add a dash of cayenne to the sauce.

1 cup chopped onion
1 garlic clove, minced
2 tablespoons oil
3 cans (8 ounces each)
   tomato sauce
1 can (3 or 4 ounces)
   green chilies, diced
   or sliced

1 dozen corn tortillas
2 cups grated Monterey
   Jack cheese
1 cup sour cream

Sauté onion and garlic in oil. Add tomato sauce and green chilies. Cut tortillas in quarters and arrange in a layer in a 2-quart round baking dish. Spoon on some sauce and sprinkle with cheese. Repeat until dish is filled, ending with cheese. Spread a thin layer of sour cream on top. Bake at 350° for 30 minutes, or until bubbly.   *Serves 6.*

CHALUPAS

"This must be prepared the day ahead in order for the flavors to blend properly. It looks elegant, and just needs to be heated up before a meal, so it's great for company."

1 onion, diced
1 green pepper, diced
1 garlic clove, minced
Oil
2 to 3 cups heavy
   cream
1 small can (3 or 4
   ounces) green chilies,
   diced

1 dozen corn tortillas
2 cups diced or
   shredded cooked
   chicken
1 cup grated Monterey
   Jack cheese
Sour cream (optional)

(Cont'd)

Sauté onion, pepper, and garlic in a small amount of oil. Add cream and diced green chilies. Heat to warm; do not boil. Place one tortilla in the cream mixture just long enough to soften, about 4 to 5 minutes. Remove to a large plate or pie tin. Place a small amount of chicken on the tortilla, roll up as you would a crêpe, and place seam-side down in a baking dish. Continue until all the tortillas are filled and rolled. Pour the remaining cream mixture over all. Sprinkle with cheese. Cover with plastic wrap or foil, and refrigerate overnight. Before baking, allow to return to room temperature. Bake for 30 to 45 minutes at 350°. If desired, spread with sour cream the last 5 or 10 minutes of baking. *Serves 4.*

TOSTADOS

"About five years ago, I put on a luncheon for the PTA, and made tostados. I figured on two tostados per person — but when I started serving, three men had six each and several of the ladies had three each, and I had to scramble around in the back of the refrigerator to find more ingredients!"

6 corn tortillas	Chopped tomatoes
Oil	Chopped onions
1 cup refried beans	Shredded lettuce
1 to 1½ cups thinly	Sliced black olives
sliced cooked	(optional)
chicken, pork, or beef	Sour cream (optional)
1 cup shredded	1 ripe avocado, peeled
Monterey Jack cheese	and sliced

Fry the tortillas one at a time in hot oil until crisp. Drain on paper towels. Spread a thin layer of beans on each tortilla. Top with some meat and cheese. Place in hot oven for a minute or two, until cheese melts. Remove and top with remaining ingredients. Serve with Salsa Picante (page 76). *Serves 6.*

CHANDLER CHILI

Freezes beautifully and tastes even better the second time around.
Experiment with the amounts of ingredients to find the
combination that appeals most to your family.

½ pound dry pinto
  beans
6 cups canned stewed
  tomatoes
1 pound green
  peppers, chopped
1½ pounds onions,
  chopped
1½ tablespoons oil
2 garlic cloves, crushed

½ cup butter
2½ pounds coarsely
  ground chuck
1 pound coarsely
  ground pork
⅓ cup chili powder
1 tablespoon salt (or to
  taste)
1½ teaspoons pepper

Pick over beans and wash them. Soak overnight covered with 2
inches of water. Simmer covered in water until tender. Add
tomatoes and continue to simmer. Sauté green peppers and
onions in oil. Add garlic and transfer to the pot with the
beans. Melt butter in a large frying pan and sauté meats. Drain
fat and add chili powder, salt, and pepper. Transfer to the pot
with the beans. Simmer for 1½ hours, covered.

Makes 6 quarts.

LOUISIANA RED BEANS AND RICE

*Thirty-five years ago when Ann's husband, Gary (a New
Orleans native), came a-courting to the south Texas border town
of Brownsville, he was quite unfamiliar with Mexican food. "I
admit that my family played more than a few tricks on him in
the form of jalapeño peppers ('Here, try this little green
vegetable!'), barbecued kid, and a rich soup called Menudo,
which, among other ingredients, includes tripe. This romance
endured, and I've tried to make it up to him by learning to cook
some of his Louisiana favorites. Red beans and rice was served
every Wednesday at his grammar school in New Orleans."*

1 cup coarsely
  chopped onion
1 cup coarsely
  chopped green
  pepper
1 or 2 garlic cloves,
  minced
¼ to ½ cup butter, oil,
  or bacon drippings
4 cans (15 ounces each)
  red kidney beans, or
  1 pound dried kidney
  beans, cooked

Salt, pepper, and
  cayenne pepper to
  taste
1½ to 2 pounds
  Kielbasa sausage
Enough hot, cooked
  rice for 6 servings

Sauté onion, green pepper, and garlic in oil. Add beans
(drained or not, depending on how much liquid you want for
the rice), salt, and peppers. Add sausage, cut in large pieces.
Simmer for 30 minutes. Serve over fluffy white rice, with a
salad and French bread.   *Serves 6.*

SOPAPILLAS

A type of fried dough to serve hot with honey or cinnamon sugar, or even maple syrup. Kids love them.

1¾ cups sifted flour
2 teaspoons baking
  powder
1 teaspoon salt

2 tablespoons
  shortening
⅔ cup cold water
Oil for deep-frying

Sift flour, baking powder, and salt into a mixing bowl. Cut in shortening. Add cold water gradually. Mix just enough to hold together, as for pie dough. Turn onto a lightly floured pastry cloth and knead gently until smooth. Return to the bowl, and let stand at least 1 hour. Turn onto pastry cloth and roll to ⅛-inch thickness and cut into 3-inch squares. Heat oil in a deep-fryer until hot, and drop in squares a few at a time, turning them several times so they will puff evenly. Fry for 2 or 3 minutes, until golden. Drain and serve immediately.

Makes at least 1 dozen.

NOTES

PATTI COFFEY
Plum Island, Massachusetts

"Someone was watching me make a pie once and observed that I made a long and tedious ordeal out of it — but that's the way I like to cook," says Patti Coffey. Her method works, too, for her apple pies are so carefully constructed that they don't collapse when they're baked.

Patti's own basic rule for cooking is that you just keep trying recipes until they are right and keep tasting something until it tastes right. But it isn't all that simple, because Patti is a perfectionist and never skimps on ingredients. She approaches cooking as a precision process, and the results are undeniably delicious.

CHICKEN LIVER PÂTÉ

An excellent hors d'oeuvre that goes best with Triscuits.

1 cup butter
1 pound chicken livers
1 medium onion, sliced
½ teaspoon curry powder

½ teaspoon paprika
⅛ teaspoon salt
⅛ teaspoon black pepper
Dash of garlic powder

Melt butter in saucepan. Cook chicken livers, onion, and seasonings in butter over medium heat until onions are soft. Blend in blender in small amounts until entire mixture is smooth. Pour into a 9x5-inch loaf pan, cover with aluminum foil, and refrigerate 8 hours or overnight before serving.

Makes about 2 cups.

LOBSTER QUICHE

An extra-special quiche. The delicate lobster flavor comes through and is complemented by just the right combination of cheese and onion.

1 cup cut-up lobster meat
1 cup shredded Swiss cheese
⅓ cup minced onion
9-inch pastry shell, unbaked

4 eggs
2 cups light cream
½ teaspoon salt
⅛ teaspoon cayenne pepper
Dash of parsley flakes

Sprinkle lobster, cheese, and onion into pastry shell. Beat eggs. Pour cream into eggs, add seasonings and parsley flakes, and mix well. Pour into pastry shell. Bake for 15 minutes at 425°, then reduce heat to 300°. Bake 35 to 45 minutes or until knife inserted one inch from the edge comes out clean. Let quiche stand 10 minutes before serving.

Serves 6.

SCALLOPED OYSTERS CORMIER

With its half pound of butter and pint each of oysters and cream, this dish is not a low-calorie or low-budget operation. But it is guaranteed to make the fussiest gourmet sigh with pleasure.

1 loaf French bread
½ pound Ritz crackers
½ pound butter
1 pint all-purpose or
   light cream
1 teaspoon salt
½ teaspoon black
   pepper
½ to 1 cup dehydrated
   parsley flakes
1½ pints milk
   (approximately)
1 pint oysters

Slice bread 1 inch thick and cut slices into cubes. Grind crackers, melt butter, and mix together. In a large bowl, mix bread and two thirds of the cracker-butter mixture. Add cream, salt, pepper, and parsley flakes. Slowly add milk and allow mixture to absorb it; mixture should be the consistency of a bread pudding. Add oysters to mixture. Pour into a buttered 2-quart casserole or soufflé dish. Top with remaining cracker-butter mixture. Bake at 350° for 1 hour, 15 minutes.

Serves 6-8.

TOURTIÈRE (Pork Pie)

A traditional French-Canadian holiday meat pie, delicately spiced and seasoned. Serve with a sauce on the side.

Filling:

2 to 3 medium
potatoes, boiled and
mashed
1½ pounds ground
pork
½ pound ground beef
2 medium onions,
minced
1 tablespoon salt

½ teaspoon pepper
⅛ to ½ teaspoon
ground cloves (to
taste)
1 garlic clove, minced
½ teaspoon cinnamon
¾ cup water

Combine ingredients, and brown in large skillet. Do not overcook. Drain fat. Make upper and lower crusts for 2 pies. Fill bottom crust with meat filling, cover with top crust, and bake at 400° for 10 minutes; then reduce heat to 350° and bake 40 minutes more. *Enough filling for 2 pies.*

Pastry:

2 cups flour
¾ teaspoon salt
¾ cup Crisco
shortening

2 tablespoons butter
1 egg, beaten
3 tablespoons cold
water

Sift together flour and salt. Cut in Crisco and butter. Stir in egg with cold water. Shape dough into a ball. Chill at least 30 minutes; roll out. *Enough for a double-crust pie.*

APPLE PIE

Patti is the kind of cook who cuts her pie apples into identical slices and then arranges them one by one in concentric circles inside the crust. She prefers using Gravensteins because they are tart and hold their shape well.

Pastry for 2-crust pie
  (page 90)
6 to 7 tart apples
½ cup sugar
1 tablespoon
  cinnamon, or to taste

Nutmeg
3 pats butter
1 egg, beaten
Sugar

In a pastry shell, layer sliced apples in a circular fashion. Mix together ½ cup sugar and cinnamon, and sprinkle some of the mixture over each layer. Sprinkle nutmeg over top layer, and dot with pats of butter. Top with a slashed pie crust, and crimp edges. Brush top crust with a little beaten egg and sprinkle sugar over top. Bake at 425° for 15 minutes, then at 350° for 30 to 40 minutes more.   *Serves 6-8.*

PECAN PIE

A rich, sweet and attractive dessert, appropriate for any occasion. Top with vanilla ice cream . . . heavenly.

3 eggs
⅔ cup sugar
⅓ teaspoon salt
⅓ cup butter, melted

1 cup dark corn syrup
1 cup pecan halves
9-inch pastry shell,
  unbaked

Beat eggs with rotary beater. Add sugar, salt, butter, corn syrup, and pecan halves. Pour into pastry-lined pan. Bake at 375° for 20 minutes, then 350° for 15 to 25 minutes more, until filling is set and pastry is nicely browned.   *Serves 6-8.*

PIE CRUST

The pastry for Patti's pies is a variation she has developed to make the dough easier to handle. "The baking powder helps keep it soft, and I add enough water to make the dough elastic and moist. The idea of using only a little water is bunk. I handle pie-crust dough for a long time and work in flour until it feels right." Her pies look picture-perfect when she's through, and the crusts don't shrink during baking.

4 cups flour	½ teaspoon baking
2 cups Crisco shortening	powder
1 tablespoon sugar	1 cup cold water
1 teaspoon salt	

With pastry cutter, mix flour, shortening, sugar, salt, and baking powder. Slowly add cold water and mix well until mixture forms into a ball. Refrigerate at least an hour before rolling on a well-floured surface.   *Makes four 9-inch shells.*

FRENCH CHEESECAKE

Lighter than most cheesecakes, this rises and browns slightly while cooking, giving it a very special appearance. Tastes best if made a few days ahead of time.

Crust:

½ cup soft butter	1 egg yolk
1 cup flour	2 tablespoons sugar

Have butter at room temperature. With hands, mix flour with butter until blended. Add egg yolk and sugar and blend again. Press half of pastry onto the bottom of 9-inch springform pan. (Butter fingers to prevent sticking.) Bake at 400° for 8 to 10 minutes or until lightly browned. Cool. Press remaining pastry

(Cont'd)

along side of the rim, going about halfway up. Refrigerate while making the filling.

Filling:

3 packages (8 ounces each) cream cheese	¼ cup sweet cream
4 eggs, separated	¼ cup sour cream
1 tablespoon flour	1 teaspoon vanilla
½ cup sugar	¼ teaspoon salt

Have cheese and eggs at room temperature. Cream cheese until it is soft. Add flour and sugar; mix well. Beat in egg yolks, sweet and sour cream, and vanilla. Beat egg whites with salt until stiff but not dry. Fold into cheese mixture. Pour into prepared crust. Bake at 350° for 50 minutes or until firm. Turn oven off but leave cheesecake in oven for half an hour with door slightly open. Remove and allow to cool for at least 1 hour before refrigerating. Top with favorite fruit topping.

Serves 10-12.

MYRIAH'S APRICOT BRANDY

Exquisite in color and subtly tart, an elegant after-dinner drink.

1½ pounds dried apricots	1 quart vodka
1 pound sugar (1¾ cups)	

Place (do not mix) ingredients in a half-gallon *flat*-topped glass jar. Turn the jar twice a day (allowing jar to set on its top for half the day) for 8 days — and your first batch is ready. You may use the same apricots (more sugar and vodka) to make more — only let the second batch set for 12 to 14 days.

Makes 1 quart.

SUSIE CROSS
Barrington, Rhode Island

Christmas begins in September each year at the Cross household, when Susie begins planning her Christmas baking and candy-making. The grocery budget increases perceptibly each week by the price of an extra sack of flour, a pound of sweet butter or nuts, a box of confectioners sugar, a bag of chocolate chips. Then early in October, Susie begins baking — no mean project, for each year she bakes one hundred dozen cookies (of twenty different varieties) and hand-dips dozens of chocolates as gifts for friends, relatives, and business associates.

Susie keeps a Christmas baking notebook, listing the types of cookies she makes each year (along with comments on their popularity), and the kind of gift box used. Each year she repeats a few favorite recipes and adds some new ones, scouring cookbooks year-round for novel recipes or adapting part of one recipe to another. She's fussy about ingredients, insisting on the best quality, and is painstaking in her methods. "Baking is very precise," she says. "If you alter the proportions of ingredients very much, you're likely to have a disaster. In a cookie recipe, for instance, if you substitute brown sugar for white, you may end up with a dough that smears all over the cookie sheet, because brown sugar contains more moisture than white. Hors d'oeuvres and main dishes are much more flexible, and you can be more spontaneous with them."

How to Make
Hand-Dipped Chocolates

There is a knack — or maybe about a dozen knacks — to dipping chocolates. To begin with, it is important to have an accurate candy thermometer, for the temperature of the melted chocolate is critical. The chocolate is melted in a double boiler over hot water, and no water should accidentally drip into the chocolate, for even a couple of drops could ruin a batch of chocolate.

Susie makes the buttercream and peanut butter centers for her candies ahead of time and keeps them, well wrapped, in her refrigerator. They should be brought to room temperature for dipping.

When she can find it, Susie uses special candy-maker's chocolate, which has an exceptionally even texture, but most of the time she buys eighteen-ounce packages of Nestle's semi-sweet chocolate chips. "Always use good chocolate — never chocolate-flavored chips or other imitations — and always work with at least a pound of chocolate at a time."

Susie places the chips in the top of a glass double boiler over hot water and constantly monitors the temperature of the chocolate as it begins to melt. "Heat the melted chocolate to 105°, then add cold water to the bottom of the double boiler to bring the temperature of the chocolate down to 80°. Then add hot water to the bottom pot to bring the chocolate back up to 85° for dipping. It shouldn't be too runny," she warns. Melting and cooling the chocolate, then reheating it slightly, tempers it and ensures that the chocolate will set up quickly and have a nice shine. Milk chocolate can be used for dipping as well, but in that case, bring the chocolate back up to 88°-90° for dipping.

Susie uses the double-boiler top for dipping; if the glossy chocolate cools off too much, she rewarms it over hot water. Her dipping utensil is a favorite two-pronged pickle fork (fingers also work well, she notes). She tosses the centers into the pot one at a time, covers them with chocolate, and gently lifts them out with the fork. The dipped candies are set on waxed paper to cool at room temperature, unless the weather is very hot and humid, in which case they can be set in the refrigerator to cool.

"The candy should set up in about fifteen minutes," says Susie, "if the chocolate is good and the air is dry and cool. If the candy is setting up properly, the chocolate won't settle to the bottom of the piece."

Susie often freezes the chocolates after they have set up, wrapping each piece individually. She states that chocolates won't turn gray from freezing as long as the candy is thawed out while still wrapped.

The hardest part of candy-making comes at the very end: "The candies should ripen for two or three days," says Susie. "Don't eat them the first day."

BUTTERCREAM CENTERS

These rich, creamy centers produce chocolates of the finest quality. Dipped candies can be refrigerated for two months or frozen for six months. Let them stand, wrapped, at room temperature for two hours if refrigerated and eight hours if frozen before opening the package. Do not freeze undipped centers.

3 cups sugar
1 cup water
¼ teaspoon cream of
  tartar
⅛ teaspoon baking
  soda, dissolved in ½
  teaspoon hot water

¼ cup (or less) very soft
  butter
¼ teaspoon salt
1 teaspoon vanilla
¼ cup chopped nuts
  (optional)

In a 2-quart saucepan, cook sugar, 1 cup water, and cream of tartar to 238°-240°. Wash sides of pan from time to time with a brush dipped in cool water. Remove from heat, and add baking soda dissolved in hot water. Do not stir. Pour at once onto cool marble or heavy stainless-steel cookie sheet wiped with a damp cloth. Let mixture stand for 10 to 12 minutes, until syrup feels lukewarm (110°-115°). Cream with a spatula or a 3-inch paint scraper for 5 minutes. Then add butter, salt, and vanilla, and work them into the mixture until it is cool and thick. It should take 12 to 15 minutes. When candy holds its shape and is no longer stringy, knead it for about 1 minute, but don't overmix. Small lumps will soften. Add ¼ cup chopped nuts, if desired, while kneading. Wrap in waxed paper and keep cool. *(Note:* If buttercream doesn't hold its shape after working for 15 minutes, let it sit undisturbed for 15 minutes longer, then check. If it holds its shape, put it in a bowl, without kneading, and refrigerate.) When ready to dip, shape into balls or ovals. Place on waxed paper and let stand for 30 minutes but no more than 2 hours. (If centers are to be dipped

(Cont'd)

more than 24 hours after cooking, cook to 240°. Wrap well, chill, and remove from refrigerator 1 hour before shaping to soften.)   *Makes 80-100 centers.*

FLAVORED BUTTERCREAM CENTERS

Raspberry: Omit vanilla, and add instead 1 teaspoon or more raspberry extract, ½ teaspoon lemon extract, and ⅛ teaspoon red food coloring.

Lemon: Omit vanilla, and add instead 1 tablespoon (or to taste) lemon flavoring and ⅛ teaspoon yellow food coloring.

Orange: Substitute orange extract and coloring for lemon.

Maple: Add 1 teaspoon maple flavoring and 1 tablespoon dark melted dipping chocolate. Add ¼ cup chopped nuts.

PEANUT BUTTER SQUARES

Outstanding — and so easy to make. Dipped in chocolate, they taste like chocolate-coated peanut butter fudge.

¼ cup butter	1 teaspoon vanilla
⅓ cup chunky peanut butter	1 box (1 pound) confectioners sugar
½ cup light corn syrup	⅓ cup instant nonfat dry milk powder
1 tablespoon water	

Butter an 8-inch square pan. In the top of a double boiler over boiling water combine butter and peanut butter. Stir until butter melts. Add corn syrup, water, and vanilla. Mix well. Combine sugar and dry milk, and gradually add to peanut butter mixture. Heat over boiling water until smooth. Pour into pan. Cool before cutting into squares.

Makes 36 large or 72 small centers for dipping.

MELTAWAYS

Susie uses sweet (unsalted) butter in baking — a legacy from her childhood on a dairy farm, where she learned to appreciate pure, fresh dairy products and other farm produce. "When we were growing up, my father really made a lot out of birthdays and holidays. At Christmastime, when the pressures of farming were less, he made gingerbread houses and baked cookies — it was very festive!" And so are these mouthwatering treats, with buttercream frosting sandwiched in between.

1 cup butter	¾ cup finely chopped
1½ cups confectioners	walnuts
sugar	1 cup Buttercream
1 teaspoon vanilla	Frosting tinted green
1½ cups flour	and pink (page 102)

Cream butter and ½ cup confectioners sugar until fluffy and light. Stir in vanilla and mix well. Add flour and nuts and blend to make a stiff dough. (Add up to ¼ cup more flour to stiffen dough.) Roll dough a teaspoonful at a time into small balls. Place 1 inch apart on a lightly greased cookie sheet and bake at 350° for 12 to 15 minutes, until firm. Roll in remaining 1 cup confectioners sugar while still warm. ("I push them all together on the cookie sheet and cover them with the sugar pushed through a sieve.") Cool on a rack. Sandwich cookies with frosting in between, using a spatula or cake decorating set fitted with a star tip. (If cookies are to be frozen, do not frost until they are thawed and ready to be served.) *Makes 2½ dozen.*

COCONUT CHOCOLATE MERINGUE BARS

"Before freezing soft bars like these, I wrap them individually in plastic wrap. It takes time, but the bars stay soft and fresh. Leave them wrapped until ready to serve."

¾ cup butter
½ cup brown sugar
½ cup granulated
   sugar
3 eggs, separated
1 teaspoon vanilla
2 cups flour
1 teaspoon baking
   powder
¼ teaspoon baking soda
¼ teaspoon salt
1 package (6 ounces)
   chocolate chips
1 cup flaked coconut
¾ cup coarsely
   chopped nuts
1 cup brown sugar

Blend butter, ½ cup brown sugar, granulated sugar, egg yolks, and vanilla. Beat until well blended and smooth. Stir in flour, baking powder, soda, and salt. Spread dough in a greased 13x9-inch pan, spreading it to make an even layer. Sprinkle the top of the dough with chocolate chips, coconut, and nuts. Beat egg whites until foamy. Beat in 1 cup brown sugar, a tablespoon at a time, and continue beating until stiff and glossy, about 3 minutes. Spread meringue on top of dough, distributing it gently but evenly. Bake at 350° for 35 to 40 minutes. Cool and cut into bars.   *Makes about 2 dozen.*

CHOCOLATE BUTTERSWEETS

Very rich and buttery. These cookies do not freeze well.

Dough:

1 cup butter	2 teaspoons vanilla
1 cup confectioners sugar	2 to 2½ cups flour
½ teaspoon salt	

Cream butter, and add sugar, salt, and vanilla. Mix well. Stir in flour. Shape by teaspoonfuls into balls on an ungreased cookie sheet. Press a hole in the center of each cookie with your thumb or fingertip. Bake at 350° for 12 to 15 minutes, until firm and light brown. Prepare filling and frosting as cookies bake. Fill while warm; spread with cooled frosting.

Makes about 3 dozen.

Filling:

6 ounces cream cheese, softened	4 tablespoons flour
2 cups confectioners sugar	2 teaspoons vanilla
	1 cup chopped nuts
	1 cup coconut

Combine first 4 ingredients and cream well. Stir in nuts and coconut.

Frosting:

1 cup chocolate chips	1 cup confectioners sugar
2 tablespoons butter	
2 tablespoons water	

Melt chocolate chips, butter, and water over low heat, stirring constantly. Stir in confectioners sugar and beat until smooth.

ISCHLER COOKIES

These taste great, but are not good to give as gifts because they must be kept refrigerated.

8 ounces blanched, ground almonds
2¼ cups flour
⅔ cup sugar
¼ teaspoon almond extract
1¼ cups cold butter, cut into slices

¾ cup smooth, thick apricot jam (12-ounce jar)
12 ounces chocolate chips
2 tablespoons Crisco shortening

Combine nuts, flour, sugar, and almond extract in a large bowl. Cut in butter until mixture resembles coarse meal. Or place all ingredients in a food processor and combine, using a rapid on-off action. Turn dough out onto a board and form it into a ball. Work the dough by pushing it away from you with the heel of your hand. Do this twice. Divide the dough in half. Roll each half between sheets of waxed paper to ¼-inch thickness. Slide a cookie sheet under the waxed paper, and chill dough in refrigerator or freeze until firm. Remove top waxed paper, and cut dough into rounds with 1½- or 2-inch cutter. Reroll scraps, chill, and cut. Place cutout dough on ungreased cookie sheets. Bake at 350° for 12 to 15 minutes, until firm and golden. Leave on cookie sheets for a minute or two before removing to racks to cool. Sandwich cookies with jam. Melt together chocolate chips and Crisco over hot water, transfer to bowl, and dip half of each sandwich into glaze. Cool on waxed-paper-lined cookie sheets and keep refrigerated.

Makes about 3 dozen.

SUGAR COOKIE CUTOUTS

Perfectly lovely sugar cookies—golden in color, crisp, and light. These freeze well, unfrosted. Decorate with frostings or, if desired, with colored sugars, sprinkles, etc.

3¼ cups flour	2 eggs
1 teaspoon baking powder	1 teaspoon vanilla
½ teaspoon salt	Buttercream or Ornamental Frosting
¾ cup butter	(recipes follow)
1 cup sugar	

Combine flour, baking powder, and salt. Cream butter with sugar until fluffy and light. Beat in eggs and vanilla. Stir in flour mixture to make a firm dough. Chill thoroughly. Roll out a quarter of the dough at a time to ⅛-inch thickness on a lightly floured board or waxed paper. Cut into desired shapes. Place 1 inch apart on greased cookie sheets. Reroll and cut trimmings. Bake at 350° for 10 minutes, until firm and lightly golden. Remove to cool on racks. Spread with Buttercream or Ornamental Frosting. *Makes about 5 dozen.*

BUTTERCREAM FROSTING

¼ cup butter or margarine	1 teaspoon vanilla
2 cups confectioners sugar	Green or red food coloring
1 to 2 tablespoons milk	

Cream butter and sugar together until light. Add milk and vanilla to get the proper consistency. (It should be stiff enough to hold its shape when pressed from a decorating bag.) Tint with coloring as desired. *Makes about 2 cups.*

(Cont'd)

ORNAMENTAL FROSTING

2 egg whites
2½ to 3 cups
   confectioners sugar

⅛ teaspoon cream of
   tartar

Beat all ingredients together until thick and smooth.

Will frost about 5 dozen cookies.

FROSTED SHORTBREADS

"I freeze these before coating with chocolate; thaw them in a closed container, then dip." First-rate cookies for Christmas or any time. They are not at all hard to do, but they taste like they were made by a professional bakery.

1 cup sweet butter
¾ cup confectioners
   sugar
1 teaspoon vanilla
2 cups flour

½ teaspoon salt
6 ounces semi-sweet
   chocolate ("I use
   chips.")

Cream butter, sugar, and vanilla. Gently stir in flour mixed with salt to make a fairly stiff dough. Chill. Roll ¼-inch thick on a floured cloth or waxed paper. Cut in 2- or 3-inch rounds with a scalloped cutter. Bake on an ungreased cookie sheet for 20 to 25 minutes at 300°. Cookies should be firm but not brown. Cool on a rack. Melt the chocolate over hot water. Dip one end of each cookie into the chocolate, and chill briefly to harden. Store in an airtight container.   *Makes about 3 dozen.*

KATHLEEN DONOHUE
Litchfield, Connecticut

Kathy Donohue reads cookbooks the way most people read novels, and she has gathered an impressive collection of healthful, inexpensive, and interesting recipes. The bookshelves in her living room are crammed with more than 300 cookbooks and stacks of food magazines, and one of the many advantages of reading as much as she does about cooking is that she has discovered a number of helpful kitchen hints. For example, Kathy uses baby food jars for storing spices and herbs. "I use yellow tops for baking ingredients, green tops for everything else." She also says she freezes everything, from fresh vegetables to soup and spaghetti sauce, in zip-lock bags. "I suck the excess air out with a straw, and just stack the bags in the freezer. They're more compact than rigid containers."

Twelve years ago when daughter Maura was born, Kathy decided she wanted to stay home and raise a family. "I thought if I was going to be cooking three meals a day, they weren't going to be the same old thing — life is more interesting if you branch out a little. I started doing research and expanding my recipe collection, and we've never gone back to simple meat-and-potatoes meals."

FINNISH BRAID

A fine-textured bread, with tantalizing hints of cardamom and orange peel.

5 to 5½ cups flour	1 teaspoon salt
2 packages dry yeast	2 eggs
(2 scant tablespoons)	1 tablespoon orange
½ to 1 teaspoon ground	peel
cardamom	⅓ cup orange juice
1 cup milk	1 egg yolk
½ cup butter	1 tablespoon milk
½ cup sugar	

In large bowl, mix 2 cups flour, yeast, and cardamom. In a saucepan, heat milk, butter, sugar, and salt to 120°-130°. Add to the dry mixture. Add eggs, peel, and juice. Beat at low speed for 30 seconds. Beat for 3 minutes at high speed. By hand, stir in 2 more cups flour. Turn onto a floured board and knead until smooth, adding more flour when necessary. Place dough in a greased bowl, and let rise, covered, until doubled. Punch down and divide in half. Divide each half into thirds; shape into six balls. Cover and let rise for 10 minutes. Roll each ball into a 16-inch rope. Braid three ropes together loosely and place on greased baking sheet, tucking ends under. Repeat with other braid. Cover and let rise until doubled. Brush with mixture of egg yolk and milk. Bake at 350° for 25 to 30 minutes. (Cover loosely with foil if loaves are browning too fast.) *Makes 2 braided loaves.*

RAISIN BREAD

Kathy's favorite tip about bread-making is one she heard on a Boston radio call-in show: let bread dough rise in a bowl that is set on a heating pad at low heat. This is especially handy in the winter if your house tends to be on the cool side.

1½ cups golden raisins
Sherry to cover raisins
½ teaspoon mace
2 teaspoons grated
  orange rind
1 package dry yeast (1
  scant tablespoon)
2 cups warm milk

⅓ cup sugar
2 teaspoons salt
3 tablespoons butter
5 to 6 cups flour
Melted butter
1 egg yolk
2 tablespoons cream

The night before, plump raisins in sherry with mace and orange rind added. (Drain before using.) The next day, dissolve yeast in ¼ cup of the milk. Combine rest of milk, sugar, salt, and butter in large bowl. Add yeast mixture and, using a wooden spoon, stir in enough flour to make a stiff dough. Knead on a floured board until elastic and smooth, about 10 minutes. Place in a greased bowl and let rise, covered, until doubled. Punch dough down, and knead briefly. Return to bowl and let rise for 30 minutes. Divide dough in half and roll each part into a 20x7-inch rectangle. Brush with melted butter and sprinkle with drained raisin mixture. Tightly roll up dough widthwise, pinching ends together. Fit into 2 buttered 8x4-inch loaf pans, and let rise until tops are just above rims of pans. Brush with mixture of egg yolk and cream. Bake at 400° for 10 minutes, then reduce heat to 350° and bake 20 to 30 minutes longer.   *Makes 2 loaves.*

SUNNY ACRES CORN CHOWDER

A rich, buttery, and properly unthickened chowder, mildly flavored with a touch of thyme and marjoram.

4 medium potatoes, cubed
4 medium onions, sliced
6 tablespoons butter
4 cups milk
½ cup light cream
2 large cans creamed corn

1½ teaspoons salt
⅛ teaspoon pepper
¼ teaspoon parsley, or more to taste
⅛ teaspoon thyme
⅛ teaspoon marjoram

Cook cubed potatoes in water to cover for 15 minutes. Meanwhile, fry onions in 2 tablespoons butter. Warm the milk and cream in a large kettle and add drained potatoes (reserving ½ cup of the liquid to rinse out the corn cans and add to soup). Stir in onions, corn, remaining 4 tablespoons butter, salt, pepper, and herbs. Heat mixture to piping hot, but don't boil. For better flavor, set aside to cool and then reheat.   *Serves 6-8.*

KABISUPPE (Cabbage and Rice Soup)

Hearty and unusual — excellent on a cold day. Kids love it, too.

3 tablespoons butter
1 pound cabbage, shredded
1 cup thinly sliced onions
6 cups homemade chicken broth

1 teaspoon salt
⅛ teaspoon pepper
⅛ teaspoon nutmeg
½ cup rice
1 cup shredded Gruyère cheese

Melt butter in a 4-quart kettle. Rinse cabbage and add to butter along with onions. Cook over medium heat for about

(Cont'd)

10 minutes. Add broth, salt, pepper, and nutmeg; simmer, covered, for 10 minutes. Add rice and cook 20 minutes longer, or until rice is tender. Serve in bowls and pass the cheese for garnish.   *Serves 8-10.*

MUSHROOMS À LA GRECQUE

Let this tangy mushroom-herb mixture cool to room temperature, then refrigerate for several days, or serve it right after it is thoroughly chilled.

2 pounds small
  mushrooms
½ cup olive oil
1 tablespoon minced
  garlic
½ cup red wine vinegar

1 tablespoon coriander
  seeds
1 bay leaf
½ teaspoon thyme
½ teaspoon black
  pepper

Cut any large mushrooms in half. Heat oil in a large pan and add garlic. Do not brown. When oil is quite hot, add vinegar, coriander, bay leaf, thyme, and pepper. Cover and cook, shaking pan, for 1 minute. Add mushrooms and cover. Cook over high heat for 7 minutes, uncovering often to stir mushrooms. Remove from heat, cool slightly, and transfer mixture to a glass jar.   *Makes about 1½ pints.*

SPINACH LASAGNA

This can be assembled ahead of time and refrigerated until ready to bake, but allow a little more baking time to be sure it has heated through.

1 pound ricotta cheese
2 cups shredded
  mozzarella cheese
1 egg
1 package (10 ounces)
  frozen chopped
  spinach, thawed
1 teaspoon salt

1 teaspoon oregano
Dash of black pepper
4 cups (32 ounces)
  spaghetti sauce
9 lasagna noodles,
  uncooked (or enough
  to fit pan)
1 cup water

In a large bowl, mix ricotta cheese, 1 cup mozzarella cheese, egg, spinach, salt, oregano, and pepper. In a greased 13x9-inch pan, layer 1 cup sauce, 3 of the noodles, and half of the cheese mixture. Repeat. Top with remaining noodles and sauce. Sprinkle with remaining 1 cup mozzarella. Pour water around the edges of the pan. Cover tightly with foil and bake at 350° for 1 hour, 15 minutes. Let stand for 15 minutes before serving. *Serves 6.*

CREAM CHEESE FOLDOVERS

Flaky cream cheese pastry enclosing a sweet date filling.

1 pound dates, pitted
½ cup sugar
½ cup water
1 cup soft butter

8 ounces cream cheese
2 cups flour
½ teaspoon salt
Confectioners sugar

Combine dates, sugar, and water, and cook until thick, stirring constantly. In another bowl, cream butter until fluffy. Add cream cheese and beat well. Blend in flour and salt, mix well,

(Cont'd)

and shape into 2 balls. Chill dough for several hours. Roll dough to ⅛-inch thickness and cut into rounds with a 2-inch cookie cutter. Place 1 scant teaspoon date filling on each circle. Fold dough over, but don't pinch edges together. Place on a greased cookie sheet and bake for 15 minutes at 375°. When cool, sprinkle with confectioners sugar. *Makes about 30.*

CHOCOLATE PUDDING

Kathy maintains she could live forever on a desert island on a diet of boiled shrimp and chocolate pudding — her favorite foods. The combination may not appeal to many palates, but this pudding will.

4 tablespoons butter	1 cup sugar
3 cups milk	¼ cup cornstarch
7 tablespoons cocoa, preferably Droste	¼ teaspoon salt
	1 egg, beaten
½ cup boiling water	1 teaspoon vanilla

Melt butter in a small pan, and set aside. In a separate pan, warm milk. Stir cocoa and boiling water together to make a paste, then mix in 3 tablespoons of melted butter. Combine sugar, cornstarch, and salt and add to the warm milk. Add the cocoa-butter mixture and the beaten egg. Cook over medium-low heat, stirring until thickened, 20 to 30 minutes. Don't let mixture boil. Remove from heat and mix in remaining tablespoon of butter and the vanilla. *Serves 8-10.*

CHILLED CHOCOLATE LOAF

Dolce Torinese is the Italian name for this divine dessert, which is rich but light, and not too sweet.

Oil	1½ cups ground
½ pound semi-sweet	blanched almonds
chocolate	Pinch of salt
¼ cup rum	12 butter biscuits
½ pound unsalted	(Social Teas or Petite
butter, softened	Buerre biscuits)
2 tablespoons	Confectioners sugar
superfine sugar	½ cup heavy cream,
2 eggs, separated	whipped

Lightly grease bottom and sides of 1½-quart loaf pan with vegetable oil; invert pan to drain excess. In a heavy pan melt chocolate over low heat, stirring constantly to prevent scorching. When melted, stir in rum and remove from heat to cool. Cream butter until fluffy. Beat in sugar, then egg yolks one at a time. Stir in almonds and melted chocolate. Beat egg whites and salt until soft peaks form. Fold into the chocolate mixture until no whites show. Cut the biscuits into 1x½-inch pieces, discarding crumbs; fold into chocolate mixture. Spoon into the greased pan, and smooth the top. Cover with plastic and chill for at least 4 hours. Unmold 1 hour before serving by running a thin knife around the edges and dipping pan briefly in hot water before inverting onto a platter. Smooth the sides. Dust with confectioners sugar (shake it through a sieve). Serve in thin slices with whipped cream. *Serves 8-10.*

BLUE RIBBON PUMPKIN PIE

Kathy entered this recipe in the Goshen (Connecticut) Fair and won a blue ribbon — thus the name. "I like pumpkin pie nice and firm, not too custardy, so I came up with a recipe that matched my taste, and I hoped the judges would like it too. It's just a basic pie recipe, but the crust turned out well. Appearance and taste count most at the fair."

1 cup sugar
1 tablespoon flour
½ teaspoon salt
1 teaspoon ginger
1 teaspoon cinnamon
½ teaspoon nutmeg
⅛ teaspoon pepper
⅛ teaspoon cloves
3 large eggs

1½ cups mashed pumpkin, or 1 can (*not* pre-mixed pie filling)
1 cup light cream or evaporated milk
9-inch pie shell, unbaked (recipe follows)

Mix first 8 ingredients together. Beat in eggs. Stir in pumpkin and cream. Pour into pie shell. Bake in a 400° oven for 50 minutes, or until knife is clean after inserting in center of pie. Cool completely before serving. *Serves 6-8.*

FLAKY PASTRY

2 cups flour
1 teaspoon salt
⅔ cup Crisco shortening
2 tablespoons butter, melted

5 tablespoons cold water
1 tablespoon vinegar

Mix flour and salt. Cut in shortening and butter until mixture is like coarse crumbs. Add water and vinegar, mixing with fork. Form into ball and chill. Roll out to form 2 crusts. This is foolproof. *Enough for a double-crust pie.*

AVIS DUDLEY
Presque Isle, Maine

Since 1963, Avis Dudley (who becomes "Ma" Dudley when she dons her apron) has served neighbors and strangers heaping plates of good home-cooked food at her "eating place," the Dudley Homestead, where every meal is individually prepared. She loves to improvise and says she has doctored up nearly every recipe she's used, so that after a while everything she cooks is her own creation.

"I think that everyone can be a good cook if they learn to like to do it. The best way to be a good cook that I know is to first just be a good basic cook. Then when you see a new recipe, try it. If you like it, keep it. If you don't, don't bother with it."

With a few exceptions, everybody calls up at least a day in advance to make reservations at Ma Dudley's, where they can even order the meal and discuss the preparation of it. "When I make a menu I don't think of how to make a profit, but of making the things that I like the best and what my guests will like. It's the food I like to eat myself. That's very important. A lot of places advertise 'Home-Cooked Food,' but to me home-cooked food means food that is cooked when it should be cooked, and it's served when it should be served. . . . When people come here they aren't in a hurry, and they sit down and eat and enjoy their food, and they don't mind waiting for it."

115

ITALIAN DRESSING

This amount of dressing makes enough for a salad that will serve ten to fifteen people. If you are making salad for four people, put a cupful of the dressing (minus the lemon juice) in a jar and add only one tablespoon lemon juice right before serving.

1 cup apple juice
1 cup sunflower oil (or Puritan Oil)
½ teaspoon each of oregano, sweet basil, and crushed mint leaves

1 teaspoon dry mustard
1 tablespoon minced onion (more or less depending on personal preference)
2 tablespoons lemon juice

In a jar with tight-fitting lid, mix all but the last ingredient together. Add lemon juice at the last minute, and shake well to blend.

BAKED BROWN POTATOES

These are even more delicious than French-fried potatoes.

Potatoes
Melted butter

Salt

Wash and peel potatoes. Slice ¼-inch thick. Either dip in melted butter or brush with melted butter. Place on a cookie sheet, and sprinkle with salt. Bake in a 350°-400° oven 20 to 30 minutes until brown.

STUFFED BAKED POTATOES

A simple dish that is hearty, wholesome, nourishing, and delicious.

Potatoes	Salt
Cream	Cheese

Bake potatoes until thoroughly cooked. Cut potatoes in half lengthwise, remove potato pulp from shells, and mash with a little cream and salt to taste. Pile mixture in the shells, place thin slices of cheese over the top, and return to the oven for about 15 minutes.

DEAN'S BROWNIES

Possibly the very best brownies you have ever eaten. The original recipe calls for one tablespoon vanilla, but Mrs. Dudley uses four tablespoons, which she feels makes the brownies even better.

1½ pounds butter or margarine (6 sticks)	4 eggs
2 cups boiling water	4 teaspoons baking soda
¾ cup cocoa	1 to 4 tablespoons vanilla
4 cups unsifted flour	Frosting for Brownies
4 cups sugar	(recipe follows)
1 cup buttermilk	

In a saucepan, combine the butter, boiling water, and cocoa. Stir to blend, and heat until the butter is melted and mixture is bubbly. Sift together flour and sugar, and add to mixture. Beat until smooth and glossy. Add the buttermilk, eggs, baking soda, and vanilla, beating well after each addition. Pour into

(Cont'd)

greased 18x12-inch cookie sheet, and bake in 400° oven for 25 minutes. Spread with Frosting for Brownies.

Makes 24 three-inch squares.

FROSTING FOR BROWNIES

½ pound butter or
  margarine (2 sticks)
1 cup cocoa
⅔ cup buttermilk

1 package (1 pound)
  confectioners sugar
2 tablespoons vanilla
2 cups broken walnuts

Heat butter, cocoa, and buttermilk until butter melts and mixture is smooth. Stir in the confectioners sugar, beating until smooth and shiny. Add vanilla and nuts, mix well, and spread on brownies while frosting is still warm. If you are interrupted for a while when making this and find that the frosting has set, just put it over a low heat and stir until it gets smooth and shiny. Use this to frost cupcakes and layer cakes, too.

NOTES

PAT ESTEY
Epping, New Hampshire

Some people are so well known as cooks that their
baked goods are the first to be chosen from the bake-sale table.
But Pat Estey's hardly ever make it to the table! They are either
spoken for before she arrives or taken as she brings them in.

If you ask her neighbors what she does best, they will
mention her church suppers, her chili, or her chowder, but most
of all, her Christmas breads. "To me, Christmas is making
things to give people," says Pat, and the thing she makes most
is bread — not only neat loaves of white and whole wheat
bread, but quick breads using every fruit imaginable, yeast
breads shaped like Christmas trees, filled breads that look like
candy canes, frosted loaves with cardamom seed, coffee rolls,
stollen, and more. "My sweet roll dough may end up as anything!" she says. She can make rolls for dinner, breakfast buns,
and two fancy coffee cakes out of one bowl full of dough.

LEMON BREAD

A nice, moist bread, which keeps well in the refrigerator. Do not wrap until completely cooled.

½ cup brown sugar
½ cup lemon juice
1 cup oil
Remainder of 1-pound
  box brown sugar
4 eggs
½ teaspoon salt

½ teaspoon baking soda
1 cup buttermilk
3 cups sifted whole
  wheat flour
Grated rind of 3 lemons
1 cup finely chopped
  pecans

Mix first 2 ingredients together, and set aside. Grease and line 2 loaf pans (8½x4½-inch) with waxed paper. In large bowl, mix oil and remaining brown sugar. Beat in eggs, one at a time. Mix salt and soda with buttermilk. Add flour and buttermilk mixture alternately to egg mixture, starting and ending with flour. Beat well. Add lemon rind and pecans. Pour into prepared pans and bake at 350° for about 50 minutes. Remove bread from pans to waxed paper or foil on a cookie sheet. Prick holes in top of bread with a toothpick. Bring lemon-sugar mixture to a boil and spoon over top of hot bread to cover completely. Glaze will run down the sides. Cool thoroughly. *Makes 2 loaves.*

APRICOT-CRANBERRY LOAF

Very tart but so good. Try it toasted with honey for a real treat.
Best to let bread sit for a day before slicing and serving.

2 cups all-purpose
  flour
¾ to 1 cup sugar (to
  taste)
1 tablespoon baking
  powder
½ teaspoon salt
1 cup diced dried
  apricots
1 cup chopped
  cranberries

½ cup coarsely chopped
  nuts
2 eggs, beaten slightly
1 cup milk
¼ cup butter or
  margarine, melted
1 teaspoon grated
  lemon peel

Grease a 9x5-inch loaf pan. In large bowl, stir flour, sugar,
baking powder, and salt together. Add apricots, cranberries,
and nuts. Toss lightly until fruit is coated. In small bowl,
combine eggs, milk, melted butter, and grated lemon peel.
Pour over dry ingredients and stir just until dry ingredients are
moistened. Do not overmix. Pour into greased pan, and bake
at 350° for 60 to 70 minutes, or until toothpick inserted in
center comes out clean. Cool in pan 10 minutes, and finish
cooling on rack. *Makes 1 loaf.*

APPLESAUCE NUT BREAD

Serve this hot and slathered with butter for breakfast, or spread with cream cheese for afternoon tea.

1 cup granulated sugar
1 cup applesauce
⅓ cup oil
2 eggs
3 tablespoons milk
2 cups all-purpose flour
1 teaspoon baking
   soda
½ teaspoon baking
   powder
1 teaspoon cinnamon
¼ teaspoon salt
¼ teaspoon nutmeg
1 cup chopped pecans
¼ cup brown sugar

Grease a 9x5-inch loaf pan. In large bowl, combine granulated sugar, applesauce, oil, eggs, and milk. Mix well. In small bowl, combine flour, soda, baking powder, ½ teaspoon cinnamon, salt, and nutmeg. Add to applesauce mixture, and beat until well mixed. Stir in ¾ cup chopped pecans. Pour into pan. Mix together the brown sugar and remaining ½ teaspoon cinnamon and ¼ cup pecans. Sprinkle over batter. Bake at 350° for 1 hour, or until toothpick inserted in center comes out clean. Cover loosely with foil after the first 30 minutes of baking. Cool in pan 10 minutes; finish cooling on rack.

Makes 1 loaf.

PUMPKIN BREAD

One of the best ever! For an even richer bread, use a cup each of raisins and dates. Stays moist for days.

⅔ cup shortening, or 1 cup corn oil
2⅔ cups sugar
4 eggs
1 can (15 to 16 ounces) pumpkin
⅔ cup water
3⅓ cups flour
2 teaspoons baking soda
1½ teaspoons salt
½ teaspoon baking powder
2 teaspoons cinnamon
1 teaspoon cloves
⅔ cup coarsely chopped nuts
⅔ cup raisins (optional)
⅔ cup chopped dates (optional)

Grease a 9x5-inch or three 8½x4½-inch loaf pans. In large bowl, cream shortening and sugar until fluffy. Stir in eggs, pumpkin, and water. Mix together flour, soda, salt, baking powder, cinnamon, and cloves, and add to egg and pumpkin mixture. Stir in nuts, and raisins and dates if desired. Pour into pans and bake at 350° about 60 to 70 minutes. (Small pans about 65 minutes.) Cool in pans 10 minutes. Finish cooling on rack.   *Makes 3 small or 2 large loaves.*

SWEET ROLL DOUGH

The dough for this recipe can be divided into thirds: one third for rolls, another third for a Christmas tree bread, and the last for a candy cane bread. "Both the Christmas tree and the candy cane make beautiful decorative breads for a Christmas brunch or buffet. They are also popular at bake sales and as gifts."

3 packages dry yeast	1½ teaspoons salt
¾ cup warm water	3 eggs
¾ cup lukewarm milk (scalded, then cooled)	¾ cup oil or other shortening
¾ cup sugar	7 cups flour

Dissolve yeast in warm water. Stir in milk, sugar, salt, eggs, shortening, and 2½ cups flour. Beat until smooth. (You may use mixer to this point, but not later unless you have a bread-hook attachment.) Mix in enough remaining flour to make dough easy to handle. Turn dough on lightly floured surface and knead until smooth and elastic (about 5 minutes). Place in greased bowl; turn greased side up. (Dough may be refrigerated at this point for 3 to 4 days.) Cover and let rise in warm place until double (about 1½ hours). Punch down dough.

For Rolls: Shape one third of the dough into rolls, cover, and let rise until double (about 30 minutes). Bake 15 to 20 minutes in 375° oven until golden. Brush with butter while still warm, and drizzle with a thin, quick icing, made of 2 cups confectioners sugar, 2 to 3 tablespoons milk, and 1 teaspoon vanilla.

For a Christmas Tree: Divide the second third of the dough into 17 balls the size of golf balls and arrange on a greased cookie sheet in the shape of a Christmas tree. Let rise 1 hour, then bake at 375° for 20 to 25 minutes, or until golden.

(Cont'd)

When cool, frost with quick icing (see above). Decorate the tree with red and green candied cherries and whole almonds, or substitute maraschino cherries if the cake is for young people, but be sure to dry the maraschinos well.

For a Candy Cane: Pat the last third of the dough into a 15x6-inch rectangle. With scissors cut 2-inch-deep snips a half inch apart along each edge. Down the center of the rectangle spread ½ cup chopped maraschino cherries mixed with ½ cup apricot preserves. Then fold the edge strips into the center, alternating a strip from one side, then a strip from the other, crossing the ends. When it is all folded, stretch the roll until it is about 22 inches long and bend one end over to form a cane. Without letting it rise again, bake at 375° for 25 minutes, or until it is golden. Frost the top, after it has cooled, with quick icing (above), giving it a striped effect with the cherry filling.

(Cont'd)

CHRISTMAS STOLLEN

Lovely version of an old favorite. Tastes best served warm. Decorate with whole candied cherries, and use other candied fruit pieces to make leaves and stems.

1 package dry yeast	1 egg
¼ cup warm water	¼ cup milk
¼ cup sugar	2¼ cups flour
½ teaspoon salt	1 cup candied fruit mix
¼ cup butter or	Butter
margarine	Icing (recipe follows)

Dissolve yeast in warm water. Cream sugar, salt, and butter. Add egg and milk. Beat well. Blend in ½ cup flour, and let stand for a few minutes. Stir in dissolved yeast and water mixture. Beat in rest of flour and turn out on lightly floured board. Cover with clean towel and let rest for 10 minutes. Knead dough until light and smooth. Place in greased bowl and cover with towel. Let rise until doubled in size, about 1½ hours. Punch down. Let rise again, about 30 to 45 minutes. Remove from bowl and divide in half. Place on floured surface and let rest about 10 minutes. Flatten mounds and knead ½ cup candied fruit into each mound. Flatten into 2 ovals. Fold each over the long way. Press edges together firmly, so they will not spring open while baking. Mold each into a crescent shape and place on a lightly greased baking sheet. Brush tops with butter. Cover and let rise until double, about 35 minutes. Bake at 375° in center of oven for 30 to 35 minutes. Frost with Icing while warm.   *Makes 2 loaves.*

(Cont'd)

ICING

2 cups confectioners
   sugar
1 tablespoon butter,
   melted

3 tablespoons warm
   milk or cream
½ teaspoon vanilla or
   lemon extract

Combine all ingredients, and spread over warm loaf.

Carole Evans
Dover, New Hampshire

"There's a lot to be learned from food: geography, science, nutrition, even metrics," says Carole Evans, an elementary school teacher. And it's not surprising that Carole would choose food and cooking as a teaching technique, since cooking is just about her favorite thing to do. When she entertains, it's over a dazzling table; when she has a few minutes to read, it's a cookbook she takes up.

Easter dinner at Carole's house is "strictly traditional," she says, remembering the Easters of her childhood. It is a major holiday in any Greek home, and the dishes she prepares are Greek. All of them can be cooked so that no two require attention at the same time. The first course can be served and enjoyed by the hostess as everything else cooks. Careful attention to the details of menu planning always makes Carole's meals seem effortless to her guests, many of whom like to congregate around her while she works. "I need a larger kitchen just to accommodate my company!" she says.

Carole's advice on being a good cook is simple and direct: relax, enjoy cooking, and be willing to make mistakes. "Sometimes the mistakes are dreadful, but the triumphs are well worth it."

VEGETABLE CASSEROLE (Briani)

This dish can be made with green beans and eggplant, or other garden vegetables in season in any combination.

¼ cup olive oil	1 can (8 ounces)
1 onion, sliced	tomato sauce
1 garlic clove, finely	1 teaspoon oregano
minced	1 teaspoon basil
3 carrots, thinly sliced	½ teaspoon cumin
2 potatoes, sliced	Salt and pepper to taste
2 medium zucchini,	
thinly sliced	

In oil, sauté onion and garlic. Add carrots and potatoes, and cook over medium heat for about 5 minutes. Add remaining ingredients and cook covered over low heat until vegetables are tender, about 45 minutes. *Serves 6.*

PAPA'S LAMB WITH ORZO (Giouvetsi)

For Easter dinner, Carole's father always makes a roast leg of lamb, flavored with lemon and garlic, and accompanied by orzo (a pasta in the shape of rice) cooked in the pan drippings. This looks lovely on a platter with slices of lamb arranged over the orzo and sauce.

1 leg of lamb	2 cups tomato sauce, or
½ lemon	1 can (15 ounces)
2 garlic cloves	1 pound orzo
Salt and pepper	Grated cheese
6 cups boiling water	

Have butcher bone the lamb and remove all oil sacs and excess fat. Squeeze lemon juice over lamb, and put lemon half and cloves of garlic in cavity where bones were removed. Lightly salt

(Cont'd)

and pepper meat and place in shallow roasting pan. Bake in 425° oven for 30 minutes. Reduce temperature to 350° and roast until lamb registers 185° on meat thermometer and is well browned. Remove from pan and keep warm.

Add boiling water and tomato sauce to pan drippings and stir in orzo. Return to oven and bake until orzo is soft and has absorbed water, 20 to 30 minutes, stirring occasionally. Remove from oven, and cover with foil. Allow to stand 10 minutes. Arrange orzo on platter with lamb, and serve with grated cheese. *Serves 8.*

MOTHER'S LEMON BAKED CHICKEN

Carole's interest in food began early, for both her mother and father are excellent cooks. If making an unstuffed bird, try baking this with the lemon rind halves inside the cavity, and even sprinkle another quarter teaspoon cinnamon inside too.

4- to 5-pound chicken	½ cup butter, melted
Juice of 1 lemon	½ teaspoon salt
	¼ teaspoon cinnamon

Rinse chicken and place in roasting pan. Combine lemon juice with melted butter. Baste chicken with a few tablespoons of lemon-butter mixture. Combine salt and cinnamon and sprinkle over chicken. Roast in 325° oven for about 1 hour, 45 minutes, continuing to baste with remaining lemon-butter mixture every half hour until mixture has been used and chicken is tender. *Serves 4-6.*

MOUSSAKA

Carole and her husband, Joe, both admit to a passion for eggplant: "There are so many wonderful Greek recipes for it, and that's only the beginning!" This traditional Greek dish can be frozen, or prepared a day in advance and heated before serving.

2 eggplants (about 1 pound each)	½ cup each, grated Parmesan and cheddar cheeses
½ to 1 cup olive oil	

Cut eggplant into ½-inch slices. Dip in oil and brown in skillet. Put eggplant and cheeses to one side, until ready to assemble dish.

Meat Sauce:

1 cup chopped onion	1 teaspoon each, salt and pepper
1 garlic clove	
1½ pounds ground beef	2 cans (8 ounces each) tomato sauce
2 tablespoons butter	½ cup red wine
½ teaspoon oregano	4 tablespoons dried bread crumbs
½ teaspoon cinnamon	

Sauté onion, garlic, and beef in butter until brown. Add herbs, spices, and tomato sauce. Bring to a boil, and add the wine. Simmer half an hour uncovered. Reserve bread crumbs until assembling dish.

Cream Sauce:

2 tablespoons butter	2 cups milk
2 tablespoons flour	2 eggs
¼ teaspoon each, salt and pepper (or to taste)	

In saucepan melt 2 tablespoons butter. Remove from heat and

(Cont'd)

add flour and salt and pepper. Stir in milk gradually. Bring to boil, and cook until mixture is thickened. Remove from heat. In small bowl, beat eggs and add ½ cup cream sauce while still beating. Add this mixture to saucepan, blend well, and set aside.

To Assemble:

In bottom of 13x9-inch baking dish, layer half of eggplant. Sprinkle with 2 tablespoons each grated Parmesan and cheddar cheeses. Stir reserved bread crumbs into meat sauce, and spoon over eggplant. Sprinkle with 2 more tablespoons each Parmesan and cheddar cheeses. Layer rest of eggplant slices, then pour cream sauce over all and sprinkle with remaining cheese. Bake at 350° for 50 minutes. Cut into squares.   *Serves 8-10.*

(Cont'd)

EASTER BREAD (Lambropsomo)

A traditional Greek Easter bread, baked with a red-dyed egg on top, covered with two strips of dough in the form of a cross. This is a very sweet bread, delicately flavored with anise.

2 packages dry yeast
½ cup warm water
1 cup warm milk
½ cup butter, melted
2 teaspoons salt
2 tablespoons anise
　extract

3 eggs, beaten
1½ cups sugar
9 cups flour
　(approximately)

Combine the first 5 ingredients. Add the anise extract, beaten eggs, and sugar. Stir in the flour, 3 cups at a time, and transfer to a lightly floured surface. Knead about 10 minutes or until smooth. Place in greased bowl, turning once, and cover with damp towel. Allow to rise until doubled — about 2 hours. Punch down and place in 2 greased 9-inch round pans, reserving just enough dough to form a cross on the top of each bread. A red egg can be placed in the center of the bread and the cross formed over it. Let rise 1 hour, then bake 30 minutes at 350°. Remove from pans immediately and brush with butter.   *Makes 2 loaves.*

KOULOURAKIA

Butter-rich cookies that go well with sherbet, chocolate mousse, or pudding.

1 cup butter, softened
½ cup sugar
2 eggs (reserve one
  yolk for glaze)
3¼ cups flour
1 teaspoon baking
  powder

¼ cup orange juice
1 teaspoon vanilla
2 tablespoons water
Sesame seeds

Cream butter and add sugar gradually. Add eggs, and blend well. Sift together flour and baking powder, and add to butter and egg mixture along with orange juice and vanilla. Knead until dough is smooth, adding a bit more flour if necessary. Dough should not be sticky. Pull off pieces the size of walnuts and roll into strips about 8 inches long; form into twists or loose circles. Add water to reserved egg yolk and beat till blended. Brush over twists and sprinkle with sesame seeds. Bake on next to highest rack in oven at 350° for 15 minutes, or until lightly browned. *Makes about 3 dozen.*

DOROTHY FOLSOM
Cranston, Rhode Island

Dorothy Folsom's contribution to the Oak Lawn Community Baptist Church May breakfasts has helped continue a delicious Rhode Island tradition that began there in 1867. The Oak Lawn event is a true community affair whose workers attend many churches but come together to produce the annual extravaganza, where 900 people can be served within a four-hour period. "After all these years, it's down to a science," says Dorothy.

Since she was a young girl, Dorothy has been cooking good food, and her reputation as an exceptional cook comes not only from the May breakfasts but also from the Galilee Beach Club, which she and her husband have operated, along with another couple, for close to thirty years. It is an unpretentious establishment with a lovely stretch of beach at its feet. There in summer, she prepares a family-night dinner once a week, and a more formal meal on the weekend.

Given her involvement with the beach club, her home in Cranston, and numerous other social and church-related activities, Dorothy's time is full and in great demand from churches and civic organizations eager to receive her assistance.

SEAFOOD NEWBURG

Because of the cost of shrimp and fresh lobster meat, Dorothy suggests using canned lobster meat and langostino. The reserved juice may be used to thin the newburg, or heated and served as a clear broth with a tablespoon of whipped cream. To stretch the broth, add equal amounts of chicken stock.

1 pound butter	3 packages (12 ounces each) langostino, drained (reserving liquid)
2 cups flour	
1 gallon milk, scalded	
4 cans (11 ounces each) lobster meat, drained (reserving liquid)	2 pounds scallops, poached, drained (reserving liquid), and sliced
4 teaspoons paprika	
¼ pound butter, melted	2 pounds flounder, poached, drained (reserving liquid)
½ cup sherry	

Melt pound of butter in heavy pot, blend in flour over low heat, and cook for about 4 minutes. Slowly stir in scalded milk and cook until thickened and smooth.

Cut lobster into large pieces, coat well with paprika (which gives a smooth color to the sauce), and sauté a few minutes in melted ¼ pound butter. Add sherry, warm through, and mix in white sauce and other ingredients. Blend well and season with additional sherry if desired. *Serves 35-45.*

CREAM PUFFS

Cream puffs are great to have on hand because of their many uses. You can make them large or small, and can fill them with custard, ice cream, or seafood. If you want large ones to fill with custard, you will get four puffs per egg; if you want smaller puffs for canapés, plan on twenty puffs to an egg.

2 sticks butter or
    margarine (1 cup)
2 cups water

2 cups flour
8 eggs

Heat butter and water in pan until it boils up. Add flour all at once and mix until it forms a smooth ball. Remove from heat. Put dough into bowl and add the eggs, one at a time, mixing well after each addition. Shape with a spoon on a greased or ungreased cookie sheet. Bake at 400° for 30 to 40 minutes, or until beads of moisture disappear. *Makes 32 large cream puffs.*

FAVORITE FILLING FOR CREAM PUFFS

1½ to 2 cups sugar
½ cup cornstarch
4 eggs
¼ teaspoon salt
1 quart milk, scalded

4 tablespoons butter
½ pint heavy cream,
    whipped
2 teaspoons vanilla

In a bowl mix sugar, cornstarch, eggs, and salt, using a whisk. Pour scalded milk over this mixture and transfer to pan. Cook until thick. Put butter in a bowl and pour the hot mixture over it. Cool and chill.

When ready to use, combine whipped cream and vanilla and mix with the cold custard. Fill puffs. This filling is also good in Boston Cream Pie, or layered with fruit for a pudding.

RASPBERRY COCOA ICE CREAM

A very rich, dark-chocolate ice cream, with a liqueur-like flavor from the raspberry syrup.

2 cups milk
½ cup powdered cocoa
Pinch of salt
1 cup sugar
1 tablespoon
  cornstarch
2 eggs, separated

2 cups heavy cream,
  beaten stiff
1 teaspoon vanilla
1 cup syrup drained
  from canned or
  frozen raspberries

Scald the milk. Sift the cocoa and mix thoroughly with salt, sugar, and cornstarch in top of double boiler. Add the milk, and cook over boiling water for 20 minutes, stirring constantly until thickened, and then occasionally thereafter. Pour over well-beaten egg yolks; cool. Add beaten egg whites, whipped cream, vanilla, and syrup. Freeze. Beat when partially frozen. (If frozen in an ice cream freezer, do not whip the cream.)

Makes about ½ gallon.

SPICE CAKE

Sold by the slice at Dorothy's beach club snack bar on Sundays, this cake is so popular that fans have been known to walk for miles along the beach to buy a piece or two. One summer Dorothy sold 480 pounds of it!

2 cups sugar
2 teaspoons cinnamon
2 teaspoons nutmeg
2 teaspoons ground
  cloves
2 teaspoons baking soda
1 teaspoon salt

2 cups raisins
2 cups cold water
2 sticks butter or
  margarine
4 cups sifted flour
1 cup nuts

(Cont'd)

In a saucepan, mix together first 6 ingredients. Add raisins, water, and butter, and cook until bubbles appear on top. Remove from heat and cool to room temperature. Add flour and nuts all at once, mix well, and pour into an ungreased 13x9-inch pan. Bake at 350° for 40 to 50 minutes. Serve plain or with a vanilla cream icing. The cake freezes well and keeps well in the refrigerator; it also makes a good bar when baked in a jelly-roll pan.   *Makes about 15 squares.*

MERINGUE CAKE

A luscious layered cake, with whipped cream and pineapple filling in between.

½ cup shortening
½ cup sugar
4 egg yolks, well
   beaten
½ cup sifted cake
   flour
¼ cup milk
2 tablespoons flour
1 teaspoon baking
   powder

¼ teaspoon salt
4 egg whites
¾ cup sugar
1 teaspoon vanilla
½ cup chopped
   walnuts
½ pint heavy cream
1 can (8 ounces)
   crushed pineapple,
   drained

Cream shortening and ½ cup sugar together. Add egg yolks and blend. Add ½ cup cake flour alternately with milk. Sift together 2 tablespoons flour, baking powder, and salt, and blend thoroughly into shortening mixture. Pour into 2 greased and floured round 9-inch springform pans.

Beat whites until frothy. Sift in ¾ cup sugar gradually, beating until stiff. Blend in vanilla. Spread meringue on top of each layer. Sprinkle with nuts. Bake at 325° for 20 to 25 minutes. Remove from pans and cool. Whip cream and fold in pineapple. Spread between layers, with meringue on top and bottom.   *Serves 8.*

FUDGE PIE

This is the most popular dessert with members and guests of the Galilee Beach Club. It tastes like a brownie.

½ cup butter or margarine, melted
1 cup sugar
2 eggs
½ cup flour
1 teaspoon vanilla

1 square baking chocolate, melted
1 quart vanilla ice cream, softened
Chocolate sauce

Combine butter and sugar in bowl of electric mixer, and beat well. Add the eggs and beat until creamy. Add flour and vanilla, and then melted chocolate. Mix well, and pour into greased pie pan. Bake 25 to 30 minutes at 325°. The pie will settle in the center. After it cools, smooth the ice cream into the depression in the center. Immediately cut into 10 pieces, wrap, and put into the freezer to keep until you're ready to serve. At serving time, spoon your favorite chocolate sauce onto the ice cream.   *Serves 10.*

CINNAMON STICKS

Dorothy's Cinnamon Sticks — deliciously crunchy and crusty — are a favorite with the members of the Galilee Beach Club.

Use any regular recipe for roll dough. (Pillsbury's Hot Roll Mix is fine.) Cut off pieces of dough about the size of large walnuts and dip them in melted butter or margarine and then in mixed cinnamon and sugar. After dipping in sugar mixture, twist and place in cast-iron pans. (Dorothy uses the kind with 11 cigar-shaped grooves, and puts 2 rolls into each groove.) Let rise. Bake 20 to 25 minutes at 400°.

Quantity depends on amount of roll dough used.

144

APPLE CRISP FOR 60

"McIntosh apples have a dandy flavor, but Cortlands keep their color best after peeling and are the best choice when you're cooking for a lot of people and the apples may have to stand for a while before cooking."

25 pounds Cortland apples, cored	10⅔ cups sugar
2 quarts flour	10⅔ sticks butter or margarine

Pare the apples, and slice into ¼-inch-thick slices. Pack into four 13x9-inch pans. Mix together flour, sugar, and butter or margarine until crumbly. Pack on top of apples. Bake at 350° for 1 hour. If desired, cinnamon and nutmeg may be added to the flour mixture.

For 8-10 people: Use the following amounts and bake in a 12x8-inch pan:

4 to 6 apples	1⅓ sticks butter or margarine
1 cup flour	
1⅓ cups sugar	1 teaspoon cinnamon (optional)

JUDY GORMAN
Manchester, Connecticut

Judy Gorman, a marvelous cook, teacher, and writer from Manchester, Connecticut, has become a culinary Ann Landers to people around the country. She is a self-taught gourmet cook who has developed a syndicated newspaper column entitled "Recipe Clinic," in which she solves and explains readers' problems and queries about cooking. In addition, she is an expert at Northern Italian cooking and has been teaching courses on the subject at a local community college.

One of Judy's pet peeves is the notion that "gourmet" cooking has to be complicated and exotic, or that it is an "elitist" style of cooking. "One of the unfortunate aspects of the gourmet movement," she says, "is the tendency toward snobbism: use only walnut oil; heavy cream is out, nothing but crème fraîche will do; you can't achieve a proper sauce without a tin-lined copper saucepan; you absolutely cannot do without the latest chopper-grinder-slicer. Balderdash! An array of sophisticated equipment does not make a good cook. To me, 'gourmet' means honest treatment of the highest quality food available to you. Put away the guilt and bring out the canned beef broth. Doctor it up if you must, but apologize to no one. The object is to try out those new recipes. If you don't get started, you'll never know what you missed."

147

BAKED STUFFED MUSHROOMS

Mushroom caps filled with a savory mixture of chopped salami, prosciutto, cheese, and herbs — sensational!

36 large mushrooms	½ teaspoon dried basil
6 tablespoons melted	or 2 fresh leaves,
butter	chopped
5 slices prosciutto,	Grated rind of ½ lemon
chopped	1 cup fresh bread
4 slices Genoa salami,	crumbs
chopped	½ cup freshly grated
2 tablespoons chopped	Parmesan cheese
parsley	1 egg, beaten
Pinch of thyme	¼ teaspoon salt
Pinch of oregano	Few grindings fresh
Pinch of sage	pepper

Wash and dry mushrooms. Remove stems, trim off ends, and chop fine. (Keep caps whole.) In a skillet, melt butter and toss caps to coat. Remove with a slotted spoon, and place in a buttered baking dish. In the remaining butter in skillet, sauté chopped stems, prosciutto, and salami. Add herbs, lemon rind, bread crumbs, and cheese. Remove from heat. Stir in beaten egg, and add salt and pepper. Fill mushroom caps with mixture. Refrigerate, if desired, until ready to use. Bake at 375° for 15 minutes. *Serves 6.*

CROSTINI DI RICOTTA E SALSICCIE
(Cheese and Sausage Canapés)

Fantastic as an hors d'oeuvre or for a light supper.

½ pound ricotta
  cheese
½ teaspoon salt
6 tablespoons freshly
  grated Parmesan
  cheese
¼ pound Italian
  sausage

¼ cup olive oil
24 slices Italian bread
  (long, narrow loaf),
  cut ¼-inch thick
24 slices fontina
  cheese, cut to fit
  slices of bread

Beat the ricotta, salt, and Parmesan cheese until creamy. Peel sausage and crumble. Sauté in enough olive oil to cover the bottom of the pan. Drain thoroughly, chop fine, and add to cheese mixture. Brush each bread slice with oil. Broil until brown. Spread the unbrowned side with cheese-sausage mixture and bake at 425° for 5 minutes. Top each slice with fontina cheese and continue to bake until cheese is melted.

Serves 6-10.

149

GNOCCHI VERDE (Spinach Dumplings)

Spinach dumplings accompanied with a tomato and cream sauce that adds flavor as well as color. Serve as a side dish or as a meatless entrée, or for a typical multi-course Northern Italian meal, present as a first course.

2 bags (12 ounces each) fresh spinach	½ teaspoon salt
2 tablespoons butter	Few grindings fresh black pepper
¾ cup ricotta cheese	Few grindings fresh nutmeg
2 eggs, beaten	
6 tablespoons flour	Tomato and Cream
½ cup freshly grated Parmesan cheese	Sauce (recipe follows)

Wash spinach and remove tough stems. Plunge briefly into boiling water. Cook only until limp. Rinse with cold water. Drain, squeeze dry, and chop. Melt butter in a small skillet. Add spinach and cook until dry (it will begin to stick to the bottom of the pan). Blend in the ricotta cheese. Heat thoroughly and empty into a bowl. Stir in eggs, flour, Parmesan cheese, salt, pepper, and nutmeg. Cover with foil and chill until firm — about 1 hour. Bring 6 quarts of salted water to a boil. Take spinach mixture up by tablespoonfuls and shape gently into balls. Roll in flour. Drop 5 or 6 at a time into the boiling water. Cook until they rise to the top and are slightly puffed. Remove with a slotted spoon and drain on paper toweling. Serve with Tomato and Cream Sauce.   *Serves 4-6.*

TOMATO AND CREAM SAUCE

4 tablespoons butter
1 medium onion,
  chopped
1 medium carrot,
  chopped
1 medium celery stalk,
  chopped
1 can (35 ounces) Italian
  tomatoes, drained
  and broken up

½ teaspoon salt
Few grindings of fresh
  black pepper
Pinch of sugar
½ cup heavy cream

Melt butter in a skillet. Cook onion, carrot, and celery until onion becomes translucent. Add tomatoes, salt, pepper, and sugar. Cover and cook over low heat until vegetables are tender. Puree through a food mill or use food processor. Return to heat and cook until thickened. Stir in cream. Heat thoroughly and serve over Spinach Dumplings.   *Makes about 4½ cups.*

SCAMPI

A simple, succulent, special-occasion dish.

2 pounds medium-size
  shrimp
½ cup butter
½ cup olive oil
¼ cup minced onion
1 tablespoon minced
  garlic

½ cup dry white wine
2 tablespoons lemon
  juice
4 tablespoons chopped
  fresh parsley
Salt and pepper to
  taste

Remove shrimp from the shell and de-vein. Rinse under cold water and drain on paper toweling. Pat dry. In a large skillet, heat butter and oil. Sauté onion and garlic until translucent. Add wine, lemon juice, parsley, and seasonings. Drop in shrimp and cook about 5 minutes or until firm. Transfer to ovenproof platter. Broil briefly until tops are browned.   *Serves 6.*

151

SCALOPPINE DI MAIALE
(Pork Scallopini in Wine Sauce)

Tender pork scallops with an herb coating, browned in butter and olive oil. An example of the delicate flavor of Northern Italian cuisine, which Judy prefers to the more familiar cooking of Southern Italy. "Northern Italy is where gourmet cooking started, after all, when Catherine de Medici married Henry II of France and brought Northern Italian cooking to the French court."

2 teaspoons dried sage
2 teaspoons dried rosemary
2 garlic cloves
½ teaspoon salt
Few grindings fresh black pepper
Few drops of olive oil
6 center-cut rib pork chops

2 tablespoons butter
2 tablespoons olive oil
¾ cup dry white wine
1 tablespoon cornstarch
½ cup beef broth
2 tablespoons chopped fresh parsley

With a mortar and pestle, or if necessary a blender, combine the sage, rosemary, garlic, salt, pepper, and few drops of olive oil. Crush or pulverize into a smooth paste. Set aside. Remove the rib bone and fat from each chop, leaving only the eye. Slice horizontally into two pieces. Place between sheets of waxed paper and pound gently till thin. Press some of the herb mixture onto both sides of the pork scallops. Heat the butter and 2 tablespoons olive oil, and brown meat on both sides. Remove from pan. Pour off fat. Add wine and return scallops to the pan. Simmer gently 10 to 15 minutes. Remove scallops and place in warm oven. Boil down wine, dissolving bits of cooked meat. Dissolve cornstarch in beef broth and stir in. Cook until thickened, add parsley, and pour over scallopini to serve. *Serves 4.*

ZUCCHINI AND TOMATO CASSEROLE

An aromatic dish that whets the appetite as it cooks.

2 pounds fresh
zucchini
4 tablespoons butter
2 tablespoons water
1 can (35 ounces)
Italian tomatoes, or 1
pound fresh, peeled,
seeded, and chopped
2 tablespoons chopped
fresh basil

1 garlic clove, pressed
Salt and pepper to taste
2 tablespoons grated
Gruyère cheese (or
more to taste)
2 tablespoons grated
Parmesan cheese (or
more to taste)
¼ cup bread crumbs,
buttered

Wash and thinly slice zucchini. Melt butter in large skillet.
Toss zucchini to coat with melted butter and cook over high
heat, stirring continuously. Sprinkle with water and continue
to cook until tender, yet firm. Remove from pan, and set aside.
Pour tomatoes into skillet. Add basil, garlic, and salt and
pepper. Cook until slightly thickened. Pour over zucchini and
mix. Spoon into a buttered casserole or individual gratin
dishes. Sprinkle with mixture of Gruyère and Parmesan cheeses,
and top with buttered bread crumbs. Cover with foil and bake
at 425° for 30 minutes. Remove foil and brown crumbs briefly
under broiler. *Serves 4-6.*

TORTONI

A rich, creamy, frozen dessert, topped with ground almonds and candied cherries — even better than ice cream!

3 egg whites
Dash of salt
¾ cup sugar
¼ cup water
½ cup slivered, toasted
  almonds

1½ teaspoons almond
  extract
1½ cups heavy cream
¾ teaspoon vanilla
12 candied cherries

Separate eggs. Allow whites to stand at room temperature for 1 hour. Beat with dash of salt until they hold a stiff peak. Meanwhile, dissolve the sugar in the water and bring to a boil. Cook, uncovered and without stirring, till syrup reaches 236° on a candy thermometer (thread stage). Beating constantly, pour syrup in a thin stream into the beaten egg whites. Cover bowl tightly with foil, and refrigerate for 30 minutes. Finely grind the almonds by using the on/off switch of blender or processor. Empty into a small bowl and stir in the almond extract. Set aside. Whip heavy cream until stiff. Blend in vanilla. Fold whipped cream into egg-white mixture. Spoon into 12 large, paper muffin cups. Sprinkle with ground almonds and top each with a cherry. Cover tightly with foil and freeze until firm — at least 6 hours. *Serves 12-15.*

CHOCOLATE MOUSSE

Although this requires some time to prepare, the finished product compensates for the effort made.

8 eggs	2 tablespoons cognac
12 ounces semi-sweet chocolate bits	½ cup heavy cream
10 tablespoons unsalted butter	Whipped cream
	Shaved chocolate

Separate eggs and allow whites to sit at room temperature for 1 hour. Melt chocolate and butter together in a saucepan. Remove from heat. Beat yolks, one at a time, into the hot mixture. Let cool 15 to 20 minutes. Stir in cognac. Whip egg whites until stiff. Fold cooled chocolate mixture into whites. Whip heavy cream and fold in also. Cover and refrigerate until firm. Decorate with whipped cream and shaved chocolate.

Serves 6-8.

MABEL GRAY
Putney, Vermont

When Mabel Gray's friends urge her to join the senior citizens' group, she just laughs and tells them that she's too busy. Although she retired several years ago from her job as dietitian at the Putney School in Vermont, her life has become even more active. Mabel puts up 400 jars of fruit and vegetables every year and fills two large freezers with the pears, blueberries, apricots, nectarines, cherries, chestnuts, greengage plums, and kaleidoscope of garden vegetables she and her husband, Ed, grow.

Because she understands the chemistry of cooking and loves to experiment, Mabel can adapt a recipe to feed two or twenty. She has made gallons of corn chowder and racks of apple pies for Christmas bazaars, has baked chicken pies to feed over seventy people at church suppers, and has made countless dozens of raised rolls for town meeting every March. That's an awful lot of time spent in the kitchen, but it hasn't seemed to diminish Mabel's energy or her zest for cooking.

BEIGNETS SOUFFLÉS (French Doughnuts)

Crisp and golden outside, soft inside, these are fantastic for breakfast. Serve warm, drizzled with maple syrup or sprinkled with confectioners sugar.

½ cup butter
1 cup water
1 cup flour
4 eggs
1 tablespoon sugar

½ teaspoon grated
   orange rind (or
   more to taste)
Oil for deep-frying

Heat butter and water until water boils. Add flour all at once, turn off heat, and stir vigorously with wooden spoon. Add eggs, one at a time, and stir until batter is smooth after each egg. Add sugar and orange rind. Drop by spoonfuls into oil that has been heated to 380°. Fry about 12 minutes.

Makes 24.

OATMEAL BREAD

Finding most breads of this kind to be lacking in the amount of oatmeal included, Mabel developed her own recipe, using four cups oatmeal, one cup wheat germ, and always unbleached flour. "I've been using unbleached flour and throwing wheat germ into everything I bake for forty years."

4 cups boiling water
4 cups rolled oats
¾ cup dark molasses
½ cup butter or
   margarine
1 cup wheat germ
4 teaspoons salt
¾ cup brown sugar or
   maple syrup

2 tablespoons dry yeast,
   dissolved in ½ cup
   warm water with 2
   teaspoons sugar
8 to 10 cups unbleached
   flour

(Cont'd)

Mix together boiling water, oats, molasses, butter, wheat germ, salt, and brown sugar. When cool, add yeast and about 8 cups unbleached flour. Knead well. Let rise, covered, in greased bowl until doubled. Shape into 4 large loaves or 6 small loaves and let rise again in greased pans. Bake at 350° about 45 minutes or until nicely browned. Brush with melted butter to keep crust soft.   *Makes 4 large or 6 small loaves.*

POCKETBOOK ROLLS
AND CINNAMON BUNS

Dinner rolls and breakfast buns that can be made from the same batch of dough.

½ cup sugar or honey
2 to 3 teaspoons salt
1 cup butter or
   margarine
2 cups boiling water
2 cups cold water
2 tablespoons dry yeast
2 eggs, beaten

½ pound raisins
1½ cups powdered milk
10 to 12 cups flour
½ cup butter, soft
¼ cup butter, melted
4 tablespoons sugar
2 tablespoons
   cinnamon

Combine sugar, salt, butter, and boiling water in large bowl. Stir to melt butter. Add cold water to cool mixture to right temperature. Stir in dry yeast and eggs. Divide mixture into two bowls. Add raisins to one bowl — this will become the Cinnamon Buns. Add ¾ cup powdered milk to each bowl. Mix well. Add 5 to 6 cups flour to each bowl to make a fairly soft dough. Knead lightly and cover with a clean cloth. Let rise until doubled in bulk. Punch down and knead lightly.

For Pocketbook Rolls: Pat out half of the dough on a floured board and roll to ½-inch thickness. Cut small circles. Put a dab of soft butter in the center of the floured side of

(Cont'd)

159

each circle; fold circles in half and place close together on greased pan. Let rise uncovered and bake at 350° until golden brown. Spread crusts with melted butter if desired.

Makes about 3 dozen.

For Cinnamon Buns: Roll out dough on floured board into a rectangle of about ½-inch thickness. Spread dough with ¼ cup melted butter, using a pastry brush. Mix 4 tablespoons sugar and cinnamon together and sprinkle over dough, rubbing it into the butter. Roll dough into a long cylinder and slice into 1-inch segments. Place flat-side down in greased pan and flatten slightly. Let rise uncovered until doubled and bake at 350° until golden brown. If desired, top with warm honey or confectioners sugar glaze.

Makes about 3 dozen.

ZUCCHINI SOUP

This soup is equally good served hot or cold.

1 onion, thinly sliced	1½ cups water
Butter	½ teaspoon salt
2 cups shredded or	½ teaspoon sweet basil,
sliced zucchini	or more to taste
1 beef bouillon cube	½ cup powdered milk

Sauté onion in butter. Add zucchini, bouillon cube, and water, and bring to boil. Simmer until vegetables are soft — about 10 minutes. Season with salt and basil. Put in blender and whirl until smooth. Add powdered milk and mix well. (Or, cook vegetables in less water and make up the difference with whole milk; milk, however, should not be boiled.)   *Serves 3.*

GERMAN BAKED BEANS

A sweet, hearty, high-protein dish that goes well with cold cuts, rolls, and salad.

½ pound hamburger
1 small onion, chopped
2 tablespoons butter
3½ cups homemade
   baked beans, or 1
   large can (1 pound,
   13 ounces)

¼ cup catsup
3 tablespoons brown
   sugar (or less to taste)
¾ cup applesauce
1 teaspoon
   Worcestershire sauce
Salt to taste

Brown hamburger and onion in butter. Combine with remaining ingredients in large casserole dish. Bake at 325° for 45 minutes. *Serves 6-8.*

GINGERBREAD

A good, basic gingerbread. The recipe makes a lot, but can be halved and baked in an 8- or 9-inch square pan.

¾ cup shortening
1½ cups molasses
1 egg
1 teaspoon baking soda
1 teaspoon ginger

1 teaspoon cinnamon
3 cups flour
⅓ cup sugar
½ teaspoon salt
1 cup boiling water

Cream shortening and molasses; add egg. Stir in dry ingredients and mix well. Add boiling water, and mix. Bake in greased 13x9-inch pan at 350° for half an hour or until done. Serve hot with whipped cream. *Serves 12-14.*

161

ELEANOR'S BAKELESS CHOCOLATE COOKIES

Keeping a schoolful of hungry teenagers fed and happy requires skill, speed, and imagination. These cookies are just one of the many treats Mabel would prepare in great quantity for the students at Putney School.

2 cups sugar	3 cups rolled oats
½ cup milk	1 teaspoon vanilla
½ cup butter or	Coconut, nuts, or
margarine	sunflower seeds
½ cup cocoa	(optional)

Mix sugar, milk, butter, and cocoa together, and cook for 1 minute after butter melts. Add remaining ingredients and mix well. Drop by spoonfuls onto waxed paper. Let cool. Store in covered container.

Variation: Using the same recipe, leave out cocoa and substitute light brown sugar. Boil 3 minutes rather than 1 minute. Add oatmeal and raisins, and drop as above.

Makes about 2½ dozen.

MOTHER'S SQUASH PIE

Sweet, spicy, custard-like filling in a flaky crust. Mabel recorded the recipe one day by standing right next to her mother and guessing at the amount of each ingredient.

Crust:

3 cups flour	1 tablespoon salt
1 cup shortening (Mabel	½ cup ice water
uses lard)	

Rub flour, shortening, and salt together with fingers until

(Cont'd)

mixture is mealy. Add ice water, mix lightly, and roll out on floured board. (Excess crust can be kept in plastic wrap in the refrigerator up to a week.)   *Makes 2 double-crust pies.*

Squash Filling:

2 cups milk, using part cream if desired (if making a large pie, also add ½ cup evaporated milk)
1 to 1½ cups cooked butternut squash

¾ cup sugar
1 tablespoon flour
½ teaspoon each salt, ginger, nutmeg, and cinnamon
2 large or 3 small eggs

Heat milk and squash together in double boiler. In bowl, mix sugar, flour, salt, and spices. Add a bit of the milk mixture to the dry ingredients, then add eggs. Mix well with an egg beater, and add mixture to milk and squash in double boiler. Stir together well. Do *not* boil. Pour warm filling into unbaked, nicely crimped pie shell. Bake at 375°-400° for 10 minutes. Turn oven down to 325°-350° and bake until pie sets.

Makes enough filling for 1 pie.

BRUCE JOHNSON
South Lyndeborough,
New Hampshire

"I took to cooking because I like to do creative things," says Bruce Johnson, whose culinary repertoire includes dishes inspired by his German grandmother, as well as Julia Child. He has eclectic tastes in food, and although he is interested in ethnic cooking, he rarely sticks rigidly to one ethnic group in planning a menu. "I might very well serve Chinese egg rolls with a pot roast — they go quite well together. You have to cook for your own tastes and keep to your standards," Bruce advises.

"I'm always looking for ways to incorporate new ingredients and techniques into old recipes. Once you learn the chemical reactions between foods, you get a feeling for when it's all right to deviate from a recipe. The only foods you can't cook with abandon are desserts — you have to measure carefully and watch what you're doing."

On his travels through the mysteries of cooking, Bruce has discovered that there are certain techniques and special effects that make the difference between expectable and memorable food. And given his reputation among family and friends, the meals he prepares must certainly be savored long after they have been consumed.

165

MANHATTAN-STYLE CLAM CHOWDER

Fennel makes all the difference in this sophisticated chowder. The fennel flavor is subtle, barely detectable, but important.

½ pound salt pork
(the fat, salty variety)
2 medium onions,
thinly sliced
2 cups cubed potatoes
1 quart water
½ teaspoon salt
Small piece of bay leaf
1 quart stewed
tomatoes

1 quart clams, coarsely
ground (include part
of the juice if
canned clams are
used)
Dried thyme to taste
1 teaspoon fennel seed,
crushed
Salt and pepper to
taste

Cut salt pork into small pieces and sauté slowly in soup kettle. Remove pork and add onions to grease, cooking slowly until onions soften. Add potatoes, water, salt, and bay leaf. Bring to boil, reduce heat, and simmer about 10 minutes. Add tomatoes and cook until potatoes are done. Add clams, thyme (start with ½ teaspoon), fennel, and salt and pepper. Simmer for a few minutes and serve hot. *Serves 10-12.*

APPLE BUTTER

Bruce makes his own supply of apple butter each year and prefers using Cortland apples, which don't oxidize as rapidly when cut as do other varieties.

½ peck, or 5 pounds
of Grade B apples,
washed and
quartered
2 cups, or less, apple
cider
½ cup sugar

1 teaspoon cinnamon
½ teaspoon ground
cloves
¼ teaspoon ground
allspice
Rind and juice from 1
lemon

(Cont'd)

Wash apples and quarter them (coring and peeling is unnecessary), and cook until soft, adding enough cider to get them started without scorching. When the apples are soft, sieve them, add sugar, and season with remaining ingredients to taste. Simmer in a heavy pan over very low heat, uncovered, until desired thickness is reached. Stir often to avoid burning.

Makes 3-4 quarts.

RED CABBAGE (Wok Method)

Bruce uses his homemade apple butter as a thickening agent in this crunchy, sweet-sour dish, which he tops with poached apples.

1 head of red cabbage (about 2 pounds)	Equal parts of vinegar and sugar (or honey) to taste
Olive oil to cover bottom of wok	1 Cortland apple, cored but not peeled, cut in thin slices
½ cup finely chopped onions (more if you like)	1 cup water or white wine
Salt and pepper to taste	⅓ cup sugar
1 cup apple butter	

Shred cabbage. Heat oil in wok. Stir-fry onions until soft, but not brown. Add cabbage and some salt and pepper, and stir-fry until hot, but still crunchy. Add apple butter and continue to cook rapidly until cabbage reaches desired doneness. ("I like it crunchy.") Add equal parts of vinegar and sugar (two tablespoons of each to start), adjusted to your taste, to make a sweet-sour dressing. In a stainless steel or enameled skillet, poach apple slices in a cup of water (or white wine) and ⅓ cup sugar. The slices will cook quickly and stay white. Serve hot, garnished with apple slices.

Serves 6.

CHICKEN À LA RUSSE

Clarified butter is butter that has been melted and then strained to remove the milk solids. This allows foods to be sautéed over high heat without the butter burning.

6 whole chicken
  breasts, boned
¼ pound butter,
  clarified
10 scallions, thinly
  sliced, including some
  of the greens
1 cup coarsely chopped,
  seeded, and peeled
  tomatoes

½ cup good dry white
  wine or dry vermouth
1 cup sour cream
Salt and white pepper
Chopped parsley

Using a heavy skillet with a tight-fitting lid, sauté chicken breasts on high heat in clarified butter, adding more as needed until chicken is lightly browned. Remove breasts from pan, reduce heat, and add the scallions and tomatoes. Mix together and add the wine, stirring and scraping the solids from bottom and sides of pan. Return the chicken to the pan, cover, and cook slowly until the chicken is fork-tender, 20 to 30 minutes. Remove the chicken and place on warm platter. Add sour cream to the liquid in the skillet and season with salt and white pepper. Take care to warm the sauce gently so the sour cream won't curdle. Spoon sauce over the chicken and garnish with chopped parsley. Serve with noodles. *Serves 8-12.*

TARRAGON CHICKEN

Surround the chicken pieces with buttered noodles that have been sprinkled with freshly chopped parsley, or leave the bird whole and serve with rice.

1 roasting chicken	1 carrot, sliced
½ teaspoon salt	1 medium onion,
¼ teaspoon pepper	sliced
2 teaspoons dried	1 cup chicken broth or
tarragon	bouillon
¼ pound butter,	1 tablespoon
clarified	cornstarch
1 cup dry vermouth or	
dry white wine	

Rinse and dry chicken. Put salt, pepper, 1 teaspoon tarragon, 3 tablespoons butter, and a little of the vermouth in the cavity of the chicken. Truss chicken. Brown the chicken on all sides in the remaining butter in a heavy cast-iron pot. Remove from pot. Add carrot, onion, and remaining tarragon, and cook for a few minutes. Add remaining vermouth or wine and return chicken to the pan on its side. Cover with a tight-fitting lid and cook at a bare simmer. During the cooking time (about 1 hour total) use a wooden spoon to rotate the chicken to its breast, then the other side, and finally breast-side up (cooking about 15 minutes on each side). When the chicken is done (prick second joint to see if juices run clear), remove it to a cutting board to rest. Strain and degrease the liquid in the pan, and add chicken broth. Mix the cornstarch with some of the liquid and whisk it into the pot. Stir, bring liquid to a boil, and correct seasonings. Cut the chicken into serving pieces with poultry shears and arrange on a platter. Spoon a little of the sauce over the chicken and serve the rest in a gravy boat.

Serves 6.

VEAL RAGOUT

A great company dish — well worth the expense of the veal and the time to prepare. Looks especially attractive in a tinned copper au gratin pan.

3 pounds of veal rump
10 tablespoons butter, clarified
⅓ cup applejack
1 teaspoon tomato paste or catsup
1 teaspoon meat glaze
2 tablespoons cornstarch
2 cups chicken stock
½ cup vermouth or dry white wine
1 teaspoon red currant jelly
Salt and white pepper
2 egg whites
1 cup light cream
1 garlic clove, minced
2 teaspoons finely chopped shallots
2 teaspoons finely chopped chives
½ pound small, white mushrooms
2 teaspoons lemon juice
12 each, black and green pitted (unstuffed) olives
Peanut oil
3 slices of good, heavy-textured white bread, trimmed and cut into triangles

Cut the veal into 1½-inch cubes, reserving about ½ pound of the scraps. In a heavy casserole with a lid, sauté the veal chunks over high heat in part of the clarified butter. When veal is browned, add applejack to the pan and ignite. When the flames have subsided, remove the pan from the heat and remove the veal with a slotted spoon. Add tomato paste or catsup, meat glaze, and cornstarch mixed with small amount of chicken stock to the pan. Stir until smooth. Stir in remaining chicken stock, wine, currant jelly, and salt and white pepper to taste. Return to the heat and stir until the mixture boils. Return the veal to the pan, cover, and place in a 375° oven for about 1½ hours, until meat is fork-tender. Baste and turn 4 or 5 times during cooking.

(Cont'd)

While the meat is cooking, make the following forcemeat, using a chopper or food processor. With the fine blade of a chopper, grind the veal scraps twice and put in a mixing bowl with the egg whites. Add the light cream very slowly, beating at high speed after each addition. After the cream is absorbed, add salt, white pepper, garlic, shallots, and chives. Mix well. If using a food processor, put the veal scraps in the processor and run until finely chopped. Add egg whites, pepper, garlic, shallots, and chives, and with the processor running, add the cream in a steady stream through the chute, and add the salt.

About 15 minutes before the ragout is done, add the forcemeat by the teaspoonful to the cooking liquid. While the forcemeat quenelles are cooking, sauté the mushrooms in remaining clarified butter and lemon juice over high heat. Add olives. Sauté the bread in peanut oil.

With a slotted spoon remove the veal from the pan onto a platter. Spoon some of the sauce onto the veal. (Serve remaining sauce separately.) Arrange the mushrooms and olives on the ragout and place the bread triangles around the platter. Serve with noodles.   *Serves 10.*

GERMAN POT ROAST

"There are only two ways of cooking beef — rare or cooked to death. Rare beef requires good cuts from the rear quarter. Cooked-to-death beef should be made from the front quarter. Don't buy too good a cut for a pot roast, or it won't hold up."

5 pounds beef, suitable for braising	12 ounces beer
	Bouquet garni to taste
Olive oil to cover bottom of pan	2 bay leaves
	⅓ cup currant jelly
8 medium onions	1 teaspoon meat glaze
1 carrot	(Bovril Broth and
1 stalk celery	Seasoning Base)
6 garlic cloves	Cornstarch
30 peppercorns, cracked	Parsley

Brown meat in hot oil over high heat until all sides are brown. Cut onions, carrot, celery, and garlic into chunks. Remove meat from pan and add the vegetables. Reduce the heat and cook the vegetables until they are soft. Return the meat to the pan with the vegetable mixture; add cracked peppercorns, beer, bouquet garni, bay leaves, currant jelly, and meat glaze, and bring to a slow simmer. Continue braising until the meat is tender (2 to 3 hours). Remove the meat from the pan, and strain and degrease the liquid; there should be about 3 cups (boil liquid down to 3 cups if necessary). Adjust the seasoning of the liquid with salt, vinegar, and/or sugar to taste. Mix part of the liquid with cornstarch and whisk it into the rest of the liquid to make a glistening sauce. Slice meat and arrange on a platter. Spoon a little sauce over the meat, sprinkle with parsley, and serve with the remaining sauce. This can be prepared in advance up to the sauce thickening and can be refrigerated or frozen. Reheat meat in the liquid and then proceed with the thickening process. *Serves 8-10.*

BEEF STROGANOFF

"Beef stroganoff should be made with fillet. It's expensive, but there's really no alternative. If you use a cheaper cut of meat, you're just making sour-cream stew."

3 pounds fillet of beef
½ ounce dried
  mushrooms
1½ cups hot water
1 teaspoon tomato
  paste or catsup
1 teaspoon meat glaze
⅓ cup chicken stock
5 tablespoons butter,
  clarified

¼ cup cognac, warmed
2 large garlic cloves,
  minced
3 tablespoons flour
2 tablespoons chopped
  fresh dill, or 1
  tablespoon dried
1 cup sour cream
Parlsey or dill

Cut the meat into strips about ½-inch thick. Soak mushrooms in hot water for about 30 minutes; drain liquid (do not discard) and chop mushrooms. Mix tomato paste or catsup, meat glaze, chicken stock, and mushroom juice together, and set aside. Brown the meat very quickly in some of the clarified butter. Do not crowd the pieces; do it in two batches if necessary. With all of the meat in the pan and over high heat, pour on cognac and ignite. When the flames die down, reduce the heat and remove the meat to a warm platter. Add more clarified butter and the garlic; stir, then sprinkle in flour, and stir. Add chicken stock mixture, stirring to deglaze the pan. Stir in chopped mushrooms and most of the fresh dill or all of the dried dill. Stir in sour cream. Return the meat to the pan to heat. Arrange the meat on a bed of noodles, spoon sauce over the meat, and sprinkle with fresh dill or a little chopped parsley. *Serves 8.*

SPAETZLE (German Egg Dumplings)

While a teenager, Bruce enjoyed watching his grandmother cook, and to this day prepares many dishes, such as these dumpling-like noodles, exactly the way he remembers her making them.

2 eggs	½ teaspoon baking
1½ cups flour	powder
½ cup water	Grated nutmeg to taste
½ teaspoon salt	White pepper to taste

Beat all ingredients together to make a batter. Bring several quarts of salted water to a boil in a large kettle. Tilt the bowl of batter over the boiling water and cut the batter with a knife as it slowly flows out. The dumplings will be irregular in shape. Other methods also work: pipe the batter into boiling water through a pastry bag, push the batter through a colander, or drop it by spoonfuls. The spaetzle cook quickly and are done when they float. An entire batch can be cooked at once. When all the spaetzle are cooked, drain them and toss with melted butter. Serve hot. *Serves 4.*

NÜSSTORTE (Nut Cake)

Very nutty, very dense, but moist — with just a hint of rum flavoring. A fancy dessert that is not at all difficult to make. Because of the whipped cream frosting, this cake will not keep well — so serve it to a large group, or a small gathering of big-eaters.

6 eggs	¾ cup flour
1 cup sugar	¼ cup butter, melted
1½ cups finely ground	
walnuts	

Beat eggs, gradually adding the sugar, and continue beating

until light and fluffy. Mix in the nuts and flour only until blended, then fold in the cooled, melted butter. Turn into a greased and floured 9-inch springform pan and bake in a 325° oven for 40 to 60 minutes, or until cake tests done. Cool cake for about 15 minutes, then remove from the pan and cool on a rack. When the cake is cold, split it in half and fill.

Filling:

1½ cups ground walnuts	⅓ cup milk
½ cup sugar	2 tablespoons rum

Stir all of the ingredients together over medium heat until smooth, and let the mixture come to a boil. Cool, then spread on the bottom cake layer. Replace top layer.

Frosting:

1 pint heavy cream	1 tablespoon rum
2 tablespoons confectioners sugar	

Whip cream until very thick, and add sugar and flavoring. Spread on cake or use a pastry bag with a fluted tube and your imagination. *Serves 12.*

Carla (Ferry) Kardt
Peterborough, New Hampshire

Carla Kardt grew up on a dairy farm in South Peterborough, New Hampshire, and after graduating from high school began to attend art school. Then, out of necessity and with very little training, she got a job as a full-time cook in a vacation lodge in Deering, New Hampshire, and found herself putting on three meals a day for all the guests. "I don't know how I did it, but somehow I made it," Carla says. She also discovered that she got tremendous satisfaction from cooking.

"In art school I had tried different mediums," she says, "and then I realized that what really excites me is cooking. It's my creative outlet. To me, working with food means creating it for the plate and presenting it as something with aesthetic value. My first job as a cook built my confidence because I was totally responsible and was able to use the finest ingredients. I'd even dream about food, and would wake up in the morning with an idea for a new dish. I still get inspirations that way."

Carla's cooking seems to rely mostly on fresh fruits and vegetables, fish and poultry, milk and eggs. She approaches cooking with a sure but delicate hand, being especially conscious of the chemistry of cooking, the way different flavors combine and complement each other. And because she believes that much of food's appeal is visual — "people eat with their eyes first" — Carla is always aware of color and texture in her cooking. She uses freshly grated white pepper in preparing "white" foods like cream sauces, she arranges pleasing combinations of food on a plate, and she unfailingly adds garnish for color.

SWEDISH RYE BREAD

A marvelous bread — slightly sweet with a fragrant hint of orange. Makes excellent sandwiches.

2 cups coarse rye flour	Juice of orange and
1 cup whole wheat	enough boiling water
flour	to make 2 cups
⅔ cup molasses	1 package dry yeast
⅓ cup oil	(about 1 tablespoon)
2 teaspoons salt	½ cup warm water
Rind of 1 orange,	5 cups all-purpose
finely grated	flour

Combine rye flour, whole wheat flour, molasses, oil, salt, orange rind, and orange juice-water mixture in large bowl. Cool to lukewarm. Dissolve yeast in warm water and add to mixture. Gradually add all-purpose flour until dough is stiff. Kneading will be long and hard, but is worth the effort. Knead for 10 to 15 minutes, until dough is only slightly sticky. Place in greased bowl and let rise, covered, for about 2 hours. Punch down and allow to rise again for half an hour. Shape into three oblong loaves, place on baking sheet sprinkled with cornmeal, and let rise about 1 hour. Bake at 350° for 30 to 40 minutes, or until done. *Makes 3 loaves.*

IRISH SODA BREAD WITH CARAWAY

Delightful toasted for breakfast or tea — or served with chowder, soup, or salad.

4 cups all-purpose flour	¼ cup butter
¼ cup sugar	¾ cup raisins
1 teaspoon salt	1⅓ cups sour milk
1 teaspoon baking powder	2 eggs, beaten
1 tablespoon caraway seeds	1 teaspoon baking soda
	1 egg beaten with 1 tablespoon cold water

Combine flour, sugar, salt, baking powder, and caraway seeds. Using pastry blender, cut in butter until mixture is fine. Stir in raisins. Combine milk, beaten eggs, and soda, and add to flour mixture, stirring only until combined. Turn onto floured board and knead until smooth. Shape into oblong loaf and place on greased baking sheet. Slash top with sharp knife. Brush with egg and water mixture. Bake at 375° for 1 hour or until bread sounds hollow when tapped on bottom. Brush again with egg mixture while bread is still hot. *Makes 2 loaves.*

ITALIAN VEGETABLE SOUP

A savory, tomato-red soup, thick with vegetables and fragant with herbs, with just a touch of honey. "In tomato-based soups I always use a little bit of honey to counteract the acidity and enhance the flavor — it works wonders."

¼ pound mushrooms, sliced
3 garlic cloves, minced
2 onions, chopped
2 tablespoons oil
1 teaspoon basil
1 tablespoon oregano
2 bay leaves
Pinch of thyme
¼ teaspoon black pepper
¼ teaspoon salt
3 cups crushed tomatoes
1 teaspoon honey
¼ cup white wine
2 tablespoons tamari sauce
2 cups vegetable broth
2 cups cooked chick-peas
1 zucchini, finely sliced
1 large green pepper, cut in julienne strips
2 tablespoons chopped fresh parsley

Sauté mushrooms, garlic, and onions in hot oil. Add seasonings, tomatoes, honey, wine, tamari, and vegetable broth and cook about 1 hour. Add chick-peas, zucchini, green pepper, and parsley, and cook until vegetables are tender.

Serves 6-8.

MIDWESTERN CHOWDER

Superb! This ingenious and flavorful combination of creamy vegetable soup and cheddar cheese is an innovation that Carla's friends and family request regularly.

1 tablespoon butter
1 large onion, chopped
2 celery stalks, chopped
¼ teaspoon thyme
2 potatoes, finely diced
2 carrots, finely diced
1 bay leaf
1 teaspoon salt
¼ teaspoon pepper
½ green pepper, finely diced

1 cup whole kernel corn
¼ cup butter
¼ cup flour
2 cups milk
2 cups shredded sharp cheddar cheese
1 teaspoon Dijon mustard
¼ cup white wine
2 tablespoons chopped parsley

Melt 1 tablespoon butter and sauté onion, celery, and thyme until vegetables are soft. Add potatoes, carrots, bay leaf, salt, and pepper. Cover with water and cook until vegetables are tender but still solid. Add green pepper and corn and set aside. In large soup pot, melt ¼ cup butter, add flour, and cook until bubbly. Add milk and stir until mixture thickens and boils. Add vegetables and their broth. Stir in cheese, mustard, wine, and parsley. Season to taste.   *Serves 6.*

MARINATED FISH WITH SOUR CREAM

Gourmet fish! A very tasty, extra-special dish. Garnish with fresh parsley before serving, or add snipped chives to the sour cream before spreading it over the fish.

1 pound fish fillets
½ cup oil
¼ cup lemon juice
1 garlic clove
1 tablespoon minced
  onion
3 tablespoons chopped
  parsley
1 tablespoon grated
  lemon rind

½ teaspoon rosemary
½ teaspoon salt
½ teaspoon black
  pepper
½ cup flour
Salt and pepper to taste
1 tablespoon grated
  Parmesan cheese
½ teaspoon paprika
½ cup sour cream

Marinate fish fillets for several hours at room temperature in mixture of oil, lemon juice, garlic, onion, parsley, lemon rind, rosemary, salt, and pepper. Dredge fish in flour mixed with salt and pepper, Parmesan cheese, and paprika. Fry fish in hot oil until brown, then lay in baking pan and spread with sour cream. Bake at 350° until fish is done.   *Serves 3.*

THREE'S-A-CROWD OMELET

Filled with creamed mushrooms, baked to a golden brown, and topped with cream sauce flecked with bits of fresh parsley.

1½ cups medium cream sauce, seasoned with salt and white pepper
4 tablespoons butter
4 ounces mushrooms, sliced
1 bunch scallions, chopped
2 teaspoons chopped fresh dill, or ¼ to ½ teaspoon dried

3 tablespoons cottage cheese
2 tablespoons sour cream
Juice of half a lemon
Fresh parsley, chopped
5 eggs, beaten
1 avocado, peeled and cut into slices lengthwise
1 to 2 tablespoons white wine

Prepare cream sauce and set aside. Melt 2 tablespoons butter in heavy skillet and sauté mushrooms and scallions over high heat, stirring constantly. Add dill, cottage cheese, and sour cream, and stir together until cheese melts. Add ¾ cup cream sauce and lemon juice, and cook until mixture thickens slightly. Add about a tablespoon of fresh parsley. Set mixture aside and keep warm. In ovenproof iron skillet, melt remaining 2 tablespoons butter. Beat eggs and ½ cup cream sauce together, and pour into pan. Do not stir. Keep eggs on burner for a couple of minutes, until bottom begins to set, then put into preheated 400° oven and bake until puffed and golden brown. Remove from oven and place mushroom mixture on half of omelet. Arrange avocado slices on top and fold omelet, then transfer to a platter if desired. Thin remaining cream sauce with white wine and pour over omelet. Garnish with chopped parsley. *Serves 3.*

LEEK AND HERB QUICHE

This is an uncomplicated, very creamy quiche. The garlic is nice even without being sautéed. Cooked vegetables, seafood, or meat may be used in place of or in addition to the leeks.

10-inch pie shell, unbaked (use favorite pie crust recipe)
¾ cup grated Swiss cheese
2 cups sliced leeks (white portion only)
2 tablespoons butter
1½ cups heavy cream
2 cups light cream
1 teaspoon salt
¼ teaspoon white pepper
½ teaspoon dill
Pinch of thyme
1 tablespoon chopped fresh parsley
1 garlic clove, minced
5 eggs

Sprinkle cheese on bottom of pie shell. Sauté leeks in butter until soft. Layer leeks evenly over cheese. In saucepan, bring creams and seasonings to boil. Beat eggs and mix in hot cream, beating constantly. Pour mixture into pie shell. Bake at 375° for 40 minutes, or until a knife inserted into the center comes out clean. *Serves 6.*

MARINATED MUSHROOMS AND GREEN BEANS

This is especially good as a salad combined with fresh, raw spinach and croutons.

2 garlic cloves, minced
½ teaspoon salt
¼ teaspoon black
  pepper
¼ teaspoon finely
  grated lemon peel
¼ cup fresh lemon
  juice
¾ cup salad oil
1 tablespoon chopped
  parsley

¼ cup grated Parmesan
  cheese
½ pound fresh, whole
  green beans
2 cups sliced
  mushrooms
1 tablespoon sliced
  scallions

Combine first 8 ingredients and mix well. Steam green beans until tender but not soft, then plunge into cold water. Mix beans with sliced mushrooms and scallions. Pour dressing over vegetables and allow to marinate about 2 hours.   *Serves 6.*

LEMON-ORANGE MOUSSE

A refreshing, light-on-the-tongue dessert. Elegant served in tall crystal goblets.

½ tablespoon gelatin
Juice and grated rind of
  1 orange
Juice and grated rind of
  1 lemon

2 cups whipping cream
½ cup confectioners
  sugar

Dissolve gelatin in juice and rind of orange and lemon. Whip the cream and add confectioners sugar. Add the gelatin mixture slowly, stirring constantly. Spoon into serving glasses and chill.

Serves 4.

JURIS KUPRIS
Bolton, Connecticut

"You have to have the right touch to be a baker, and he has it," says Mrs. Kupris about her son, Juris. "His bread is lighter and finer than the same bread baked by someone else . . . . Bakers have to be like artists. They have to think about looks and taste all the time. And they have to take care of their bread — check it, poke it, feel it, stay with it — not just mix it and walk away."

Juris Kupris' Latvian breads are his heritage and his vocation, and he still uses the sourdough rye starter his mother brought with her when she and her husband escaped from the Russians in 1945.

Juris grew up with the smell of fresh bread wafting up early in the mornings from his mother's bakery downstairs. In 1971, he went into the army, and when he came home in 1974, his mother had bought a commercial oven, her bread business was up to 150 loaves a week, and each morning Juris' father was getting up long before dawn to mix the dough. "When I got home from the army," says Juris, "I got elected to come down here at 3 AM to be the mixer." The sticky, heavy rye dough has to be mixed and kneaded by hand, and he soon discovered that he had both the talent and the inclination to be a baker. Since then, he has gradually taken over the bread business from his mother, who still helps out but does not usually put in the same long days.

WHITE BREAD

Juris uses White Swan unbleached commercial flour. Because he bakes in such large quantities, he tends to measure flour by the shovelful. When he first started baking, it took him about 8 to 12 hours to make 150 loaves of bread; now he can make 300 loaves in the same time.

4 ounces butter or margarine	2 tablespoons sugar or honey
2 tablespoons dry yeast	2 teaspoons salt
2 cups lukewarm water (98°-105°)	1 egg, beaten
6 to 8 cups unbleached white flour	

Melt butter; dissolve yeast in water. Sift dry ingredients together and stir into yeast, adding butter. Knead the dough with your hands until it is no longer sticky, working in as much flour as is needed. Place in an oiled bowl, cover, and let rise until doubled in bulk. Punch down and turn out onto a floured board. Divide and shape into 2 loaves and place in greased pans. Let rise again. Brush with egg wash. Bake at 400° for 35 to 45 minutes. *Makes 2 loaves.*

WHOLE-WHEAT HONEY BREAD

Juris also buys whole wheat flour in commercial quantities, plus a high-gluten flour that he adds in judicious scoops. He often mixes whole wheat and unbleached white flours to create a bread that holds together well when it's cut for sandwiches. This recipe makes a good-tasting, multi-purpose bread.

½ cup honey
4 ounces butter or
    margarine, melted
2 teaspoons salt
2 tablespoons dry yeast
½ cup warm water
2½ cups lukewarm
    water

4 cups whole wheat
    flour
3 to 5 cups unbleached
    white flour
    (approximately)
Raisins or walnuts
    (optional)

Stir honey, melted butter, and salt together. Dissolve yeast in ½ cup warm water and add to mixture. Add 2½ cups lukewarm water and whole wheat flour to make a sponge and beat well. Cover the sponge and let rise until it is light and airy. Stir in white flour until the dough is soft but not sticky, adding more flour as needed. Knead well. Add raisins or chopped walnuts if desired. Let rise until dough is doubled. Punch down and shape into 2 large or 3 small loaves. Place in greased pans, cover, and let rise until doubled. Bake at 375° for 35 to 45 minutes.   *Makes 2 large or 3 small loaves.*

RAISIN BREAD BRAIDS

This is very similar to Polish babka, Jewish challah, and German stollen. They're all sweet holiday breads. The braids are made loosely, and the ends are tucked under. Just before baking, a beaten egg is brushed over the loaves to make the crust shine. Loaves can be made as large as you like. For a special holiday bread, make one large braid.

2 cups milk	4 ounces butter,
1 cup water	melted
2 teaspoons salt	4 ounces margarine,
1 cup sugar	melted
2 tablespoons dry yeast	2 eggs
12 to 14 cups	1 cup raisins
unbleached flour	1 egg, beaten
(approximately)	
1 teaspoon grated	
lemon peel	

Scald milk and water, and add salt and sugar. Add yeast to liquid when it is slightly cooled (98°-105°). Add about 1 pound of the flour along with lemon peel, melted butter and margarine, 2 eggs, and raisins; work remaining flour in until the mixture is no longer sticky. Place in an oiled bowl. Cover and let rise in a warm spot until doubled. Punch down. On a floured board, divide the dough into 6 sections. Divide each section into thirds, roll each piece into a cylinder, and braid the pieces, tucking the ends under. Let rise again until doubled, brush with beaten egg, and bake for 20 to 30 minutes at 350°. *Makes 6 small loaves.*

APPLE WHOLE-WHEAT HONEY SQUARES

Chock-full of goodness, these make a healthy dessert or afternoon snack for children.

8 ounces cream cheese	1 cup unbleached
4 ounces butter, melted	white flour
4 ounces margarine,	8 apples
melted	1 teaspoon cinnamon
1 cup whole wheat	3 tablespoons honey
flour	1 egg, beaten

Mix cream cheese, butter, margarine, whole wheat flour, and unbleached flour until dough is an even consistency. Refrigerate for 2 hours. Peel apples and shred on a coarse grater. Cut dough in half. Roll out half on a whole-wheat-flour covered board to fit an 18x12-inch baking sheet. Grease the pan and line with the dough. Spread the apples evenly on the dough. Sprinkle with cinnamon and cover uniformly with honey. Roll out the other half of the dough and place over the top of the apple mixture. Score with a fork. Brush with egg wash and bake at 375° for 40 to 45 minutes.

Makes 4-5 dozen squares.

PIRAGI (Latvian Style)

Light little buns with bacon and onion baked inside.

Dough:

2 tablespoons yeast	2 teaspoons salt
1½ cups lukewarm water	5 to 6 cups unbleached flour
4 ounces shortening	½ cup buttermilk
½ cup sugar	

Dissolve yeast in water, melt shortening, and sift together dry ingredients. Combine yeast mixture, buttermilk, shortening, and dry ingredients, and knead well, adding flour until dough is no longer sticky. Let dough rise, covered, in an oiled bowl, and make filling.

Filling:

2 pounds bacon	Dash of pepper
1 medium onion	1 egg, beaten
3 tablespoons butter	(optional)
1 tablespoon caraway seeds	

Dice bacon and onion; fry bacon and drain; separately sauté onion in butter, adding caraway seeds and pepper. Combine onions and bacon.

When dough has doubled, punch down. On a floured board, roll dough out to ¼-inch thickness. Using a glass or a cookie cutter 2½ to 3 inches in diameter, cut out circles in the dough. Place 1 teaspoon of filling mixture on each circle. Roll dough around the mixture in a crescent shape and place creased-side down on a greased pan. Brush with beaten egg if desired. Bake at 375° about 15 minutes, until golden brown.

Makes 5-6 dozen.

PIPARKUKAS (Ginger Cookies)

Excellent, crisp, tasty cookies. The egg glaze on top adds a shine and pattern to the top. Cut into stars, crescent shapes, or 2½-inch circles before baking.

1 cup butter	1 teaspoon cloves
1 cup sugar	½ teaspoon allspice
½ cup molasses	½ teaspoon nutmeg
1 egg	1 teaspoon baking
3 to 4 cups flour	soda
2 teaspoons cinnamon	1 egg, beaten
1 tablespoon ginger	

Cream butter. Add sugar, molasses, and egg, and beat until smooth. Sift together the dry ingredients and add slowly to the creamed mixture. Blend well. Refrigerate dough overnight in waxed paper or foil. On a well-floured surface, roll small amounts of dough quite thin, using a well-floured rolling pin. Cut into desired shapes with cookie cutters. Place on a greased cookie sheet and brush with beaten egg. Bake at 350° for about 10 minutes.

Makes about 8 dozen 2½-inch-diameter cookies.

194

JUDY LUND
South Dartmouth, Massachusetts

Visions of sugarplums may dance in the heads of some children at Christmastime, but in South Dartmouth, Massachusetts, the heads of Judy Lund's children are filled with thoughts of roast goose, sausage stuffing, plum pudding, and other traditional foods that evoke the essence of Christmas. Dinner at the Lunds' is a festive ritual that involves the whole family, and the holiday table is a panoply of foods: traditional and innovative, sweet and tart, light and filling, hot and cold — a delight to all the senses.

Judy is a methodical cook, and her streamlined, contemporary kitchen, which she and her husband helped design, attests to that. "I don't cook for show — I cook to feed my family," she says, "so I need a kitchen that's efficient, with oodles of storage space."

Judy calls herself a seat-of-the-pants cook. "I often make up a recipe from what I have on hand, for I like to experiment, and my recipe for yogurt coffee cake came about that way. I finally wrote it down one day and sent it to *Better Homes and Gardens* — the only time I've ever entered a cooking contest — and it won second prize!"

BREAKFAST PANCAKE

Reminiscent of a popover in taste and texture, but sweet. Accompany with citrus fruit salad, and sausage or bacon, and serve to company or as a special weekend breakfast for the family.

½ cup flour	4 tablespoons butter
½ cup milk	2 tablespoons
2 eggs, lightly beaten	confectioners sugar
Pinch of nutmeg	Juice of half a lemon

Combine the flour, milk, eggs, and nutmeg. Beat lightly, leaving the batter a little lumpy. Melt the butter in a 12-inch heavy skillet with heatproof handle. When the butter is very hot, pour in batter. Bake pancake 15 to 20 minutes in 425° oven, or until it is golden brown. Sprinkle with sugar and return briefly to oven. Sprinkle with lemon juice, then turn out of pan and serve with jelly, jam, or marmalade.   *Serves 2-4.*

QUICK ORANGE-YOGURT COFFEE CAKE

Nice light texture. This recipe lends itself to endless variations — experiment with other flavors of yogurt and try substituting nuts or berries for the raisins.

1 egg, beaten	½ cup raisins
8-ounce carton (1 cup)	3 tablespoons sugar
orange yogurt	½ teaspoon cinnamon
1 package one-layer-size	
yellow cake mix	

In medium bowl, combine egg and yogurt. Add cake mix and stir until well combined. Stir in raisins. Pour batter into a greased 8-inch-square baking pan. In small bowl, stir together sugar and cinnamon; sprinkle evenly over batter in pan. Bake at 350° for 30 minutes or until cake tests done. Cool on wire rack.   *Makes 1 coffee cake.*

TOMATO CONSOMMÉ

An excellent appetizer — not as fussy to prepare as it appears.
Could also be garnished with a little yogurt or sour cream.

4 cups chopped ripe
   tomatoes, or 2 cups
   canned
½ cup sherry
1 medium onion,
   sliced
1 sliver of garlic
1 celery knob
1 carrot, sliced
1 tablespoon butter

½ teaspoon sugar
½ teaspoon salt
1 bay leaf
2 cups beef stock
½ cup orange juice
1 cup tomato juice
½ cup Madeira
   (optional)
Lemon rind, shredded

Combine tomatoes, sherry, onion, garlic, celery, carrot, butter,
sugar, salt, and bay leaf in heavy saucepan; cover and simmer
for 35 minutes. Rub the mixture through a sieve and add beef
stock, orange juice, and tomato juice. Simmer 30 minutes.
Strain through cheesecloth and add Madeira if desired. Serve
soup either hot or cold with a few shreds of lemon rind
floating on top. *Makes about 6 cups.*

CHUTNEY PUFFS

Cheese, curry, bacon, and mango chutney create a unique combination of flavors. Serve as an open-face sandwich or as a fancy canapé.

½ pound cheddar
  cheese, grated
½ teaspoon baking
  powder
¼ teaspoon curry
  powder
2 egg yolks
2 egg whites, beaten
  stiff

8 strips bacon, fried
  crisp and crumbled
4 tablespoons hot
  mango chutney
12 slices of firm white
  bread, crusts
  removed, lightly
  toasted

Combine cheese, baking powder, curry, and egg yolks. Fold in egg whites. Combine bacon and chutney in separate bowl. Spread cheese mixture thickly on slices of bread and spoon bacon-chutney mixture in center of each slice. Broil about 4 inches from heat until cheese mixture puffs. Serve hot.

Makes 12.

ROAST GOOSE

Most grocers can supply a frozen goose at any time; during the holidays fresh birds are usually available.

Roast the bird in the oven as you would any other large fowl, but prick its skin occasionally to let out excess grease. A 9-pound bird (which feeds 6 to 8 people), put into the oven unstuffed and at room temperature, will take about 2 hours to cook at 325°. A 12½-pound goose (which feeds 12-14 people) takes 2 hours and 30 to 40 minutes. Add 20 to 40 minutes if the bird is stuffed. Your goose is cooked when its juices run pale yellow; the breast meat will dry out if the goose is cooked too long.

GOOSE STUFFING

"Some people don't stuff a goose; they just put an onion or an apple in the cavity for flavor, but we like the stuffing almost as much as the goose itself."

½ pound sausage, browned
1 large onion, minced
1 cup diced celery
8 slices firm white bread, toasted and diced
½ package prunes, pitted and cut up
½ teaspoon sage
1 cup white wine
½ cup water
Salt and pepper to taste

Mix all ingredients together and stuff lightly into an uncooked goose.   *Makes enough to fill a 12-pound bird.*

PLUM PUDDING

Make bread crumbs by whirling firm white bread in a blender or by grating it on a coarse grater.

- 3 cups fine bread crumbs
- ¾ cup dark brown sugar
- 1 teaspoon salt
- 1 teaspoon cinnamon
- ½ teaspoon nutmeg
- ½ teaspoon allspice
- ¼ teaspoon ground cloves
- ¾ cup milk, scalded
- 6 eggs
- 1½ cups ground beef suet
- 1 cup raisins
- 1 cup yellow raisins
- ½ cup currants
- ½ cup candied fruit for fruitcake
- ½ cup chopped dates
- ½ cup unsifted flour
- ¼ cup brandy

Mix bread crumbs, sugar, salt, and spices in a large bowl. Add milk and allow to cool. Beat eggs. Add eggs and suet when mixture is cool. Mix fruits together in another bowl and dredge with flour; add fruits and brandy to batter. Turn into greased 2-quart mold. Steam 5 to 6 hours. Serve with Hard Sauce or Foamy Sauce (page 201). *Serves 10-12.*

DARK PLUM DUFF

Rather than the usual Christmas pudding, serve this moist, prune-filled dessert instead.

- 2 eggs
- 1 cup brown sugar
- ½ cup shortening, melted
- 2 cups cut up, pitted, cooked, and drained prunes
- 1 cup sifted flour
- ½ teaspoon salt
- 1 teaspoon baking soda

(Cont'd)

Beat eggs and blend in brown sugar, shortening, and prunes.
Sift dry ingredients together and stir into prune mixture. Pour
into a well-greased 1-quart mold, and tie waxed paper loosely
over the mold to prevent water from dripping onto the pudding
when it condenses on the lid of the steamer. Place mold in
steamer and steam for 1 hour or until pudding tests done.
Unmold, and serve hot with choice of Hard Sauce or Foamy
Sauce (recipes follow).   *Serves 8-10.*

HARD SAUCE

1 stick butter (½ cup),   1 egg white
  softened   1 teaspoon vanilla or
1 cup confectioners   brandy
  sugar

Cream together butter and sugar. Add egg white, then
flavoring. Put into serving dish and chill until serving time.

FOAMY SAUCE

1 egg   1 teaspoon vanilla
⅓ cup butter, melted   1 cup whipping cream
½ cup sugar

Beat egg until light and lemon-colored. Add melted butter,
sugar, and vanilla. Whip cream until stiff, and add to egg
mixture. Chill.

CORINNE MORSE
South Hampton, New Hampshire

"What New England cooking means to me," says Corinne Morse, "is taking native foods and doing something delicious to them." And that is exactly what she does with every dish she prepares, for she takes a real delight in making and serving good food.

The traditional Fourth of July meal that Mrs. Morse serves her family is classic, vintage New England cooking — poached fish with new peas and potatoes — but set off with a few new ideas like feta cheese appetizers or creamy, chilled zucchini soup. She begins preparing the feast the night before by mixing the yeast dough for her Swedish pastry and assembling the appetizers, which she freezes until ready to bake. Although salmon is the traditional fish for this celebration, Mrs. Morse frequently serves haddock or another fish, which may be easier to find and not so expensive. She poaches the fish in a pan of water, flavored with several bay leaves and dill, and serves it with an egg sauce spooned over the top and garnished with fresh parsley.

"Serving special meals for special occasions keeps a family together," Mrs. Morse says. "And I do think that it is very important that a person remember his heritage. One way I do this is by saving and using the old family recipes and passing them on to my children."

SWEDISH PASTRY

*The dough for these buttery and beautifully formed rolls will
keep in the refrigerator for up to a week.*

1½ cups milk	5 egg yolks
2 tablespoons cooking	½ teaspoon vanilla,
fat	almond, or orange
2 packages dry yeast	flavoring
¾ cup sugar	½ pound butter,
⅔ teaspoon salt	softened
4 cups flour	

Scald the milk with the cooking fat, then cool until warm.
Dissolve yeast in the warm milk, then add sugar and salt.
Add 2 cups flour, beaten egg yolks, and flavoring. Stir well,
then add remaining 2 cups flour. Mixture will be sticky, but
with care it can be handled. Add a little more flour if necessary.
Roll out on floured board to about ¼-inch thickness, and
spread with soft butter. Fold into thirds and roll again,
repeating this 3 times. Place on floured foil, being sure to
cover entirely, and refrigerate. When ready to use, cut in strips
about 3 inches long and ¾ inch wide. Shape each strip into
long roll, twist, and tie in loose knot, turning the ends under.
Let rise about 2 hours, then bake at 375° for 15 minutes or
until light brown. Frost or glaze, if desired, by mixing 1 cup
confectioners sugar with 3 teaspoons water, orange juice, or
milk, and desired flavoring.   *Makes 2-3 dozen knots.*

WATERMELON PICKLE

*Although it takes time to make these spicy, translucent-amber
pickles, the enticing scent of simmering spices rewards you while
you work. Actually the recipe is quite simple — the hardest part
is just peeling the rind.*

(Cont'd)

1 medium-size watermelon	4 tablespoons crushed stick cinnamon
8 cups sugar	4 tablespoons whole cloves
4 cups vinegar	

Remove the pink, ripe part of the melon for another use, such as a fruit cup. Cut the rind into ¾-inch-wide slices, remove outer peel, and then cut slices into small squares of about 1 inch. Cover with water and cook until tender. Boil sugar and vinegar 10 minutes. Add spices tied in a cheesecloth bag and simmer about 1 hour. Add drained watermelon pieces and simmer another hour. Remove spice bag and pour watermelon and syrup into hot sterilized jars. Cap and store in a cool place.

Makes 4-5 pints.

FETA CHEESE APPETIZERS

"I usually freeze these before baking them. They can go from the freezer into the oven, and that way the filling won't seep out."

½ pound cream cheese	1 package Greek phyllo pastry
½ pound feta cheese	1 stick butter, melted
2 to 2½ tablespoons cream or milk	

Blend the cheeses and cream until smooth. Using 4 leaves of phyllo, brush melted butter onto first leaf, place second on top of it and brush that; continue until all 4 leaves are buttered. Cut leaves into 3-inch squares with scissors. Place 1 tablespoon cheese mixture in the center of each square and fold up like an envelope. Continue until mixture is used up. Brush with melted butter to seal. Cover carefully with foil and freeze until ready to use. Place uncovered on a cookie sheet straight from freezer and bake at 350° until phyllo is brown and crisp — about 10 or more minutes.

Makes about 50.

ZUCCHINI SOUP

Wonderful hot or cold. This can be frozen successfully, but do not add the cream until ready to use.

5 to 6 small or
   medium zucchini
1 large onion, sliced
1½ teaspoons curry
   powder
3 cups chicken broth

1 cup heavy cream
½ cup milk
Salt and fresh ground
   black pepper
Chives, chopped for
   garnish

Cut zucchini into small pieces and place in kettle along with the onion and curry powder. Stir to coat pieces. Add chicken broth and bring to boil. Simmer 45 minutes. Put mixture in blender and puree. Add cream, milk, and salt and pepper to taste. Chill thoroughly. Serve with chopped chives sprinkled on top.

Serves 6-8.

CORN PUDDING

For a crunchy topping, mix cracker crumbs with butter and sprinkle over the top of mixture instead of combining with the other ingredients. Then bake as directed.

2 eggs
1 cup milk
1 tablespoon sugar
¼ teaspoon salt
⅛ teaspoon black
   pepper

2 cups corn (preferably
   freshly cut from cob,
   although canned
   will work)
1 small onion,
   chopped
1 cup cracker crumbs
3 tablespoons soft
   butter

Combine eggs, milk, sugar, salt, and pepper. Beat with wire

(Cont'd)

whisk. Add corn and onion, then cracker crumbs and butter. Pour into 1½-quart buttered casserole and bake at 350° for 1¼ hours. *Serves 4-6.*

SEAFOOD CASSEROLE

Ideal company fare for the busy cook — it takes minutes to assemble and cooks in half an hour. Any left over can be frozen and reheated with good results.

1 cup crackers, crushed	½ pound scallops, uncooked
1 cup canned, frozen, or fresh crab meat	Salt and pepper to taste
1 pound fresh or frozen shrimp, uncooked	1 can mushroom soup
1½ pounds haddock, uncooked	½ cup milk
	¼ cup sherry
	Butter

Mix ½ cup crushed crackers with all other ingredients except butter. Season to taste and put into a buttered 3-quart baking dish. Sprinkle remaining crackers on top and dot well with butter. Bake 30 minutes at 350°. *Serves 8.*

LATVIAN TORTE

A marvelously light cake with delicately flavored buttercream filling spread between the layers. Mrs. Morse once demonstrated this torte on a Boston television program.

10 eggs, separated	2 cups finely chopped
¼ teaspoon cream of	nuts
tartar	Filling (recipe follows)
1 cup confectioners	
sugar	

Beat egg whites until frothy. Add cream of tartar and continue to beat. Add ⅓ cup confectioners sugar gradually and continue to beat until whites stand in peaks. Beat egg yolks and remaining sugar until light and lemon colored. Add to whites, folding carefully. Stir in nuts carefully. (The finely chopped nuts take the place of flour in this recipe.) Grease and flour four or five 9-inch round cake pans, line them with waxed paper, and grease and flour the paper. Pour a little batter into each pan, about ½-inch deep. Bake at 300° and watch to see when cake is done. (It should spring back when touched.) Remove from pans and cool. Spread filling between the layers and refrigerate until ready to serve. Decorate top with nuts, confectioners sugar, or whipped cream.   *Serves 12-15.*

Filling:

3 sticks unsalted	1 teaspoon instant
butter	coffee
1 cup confectioners	1 teaspoon vanilla
sugar	
3 egg yolks	

Cream butter and sugar. Add egg yolks, one at a time, beating constantly with electric mixer. Add instant coffee and vanilla. Spread between layers of cooled cake.

STRAWBERRY GLAZE PIE

"This pie will not keep well, I'm sure, but I never had an opportunity to find out, as there has never been any left over from a meal!"

1½ quarts large fresh strawberries	1 tablespoon butter
1 cup sugar (or less to taste)	Red food coloring (optional)
½ cup water	9-inch pie shell, baked (see following recipe)
3 tablespoons cornstarch	1 cup heavy cream, whipped

Hull and wash the strawberries, and drain well. Cook sugar, water, cornstarch, and ½ cup crushed berries until thick and clear. Add butter, and food coloring, if desired, to make a bright red glaze. Fill the cooled pie shell with remaining whole berries, saving 4 or 5 of the largest berries to use as a garnish. Pour cooked sauce over berries in pie shell and refrigerate until ready to serve. (The glaze thickens as it cools.) Garnish pie with whipped cream and large berries. *Serves 8.*

PLAIN PASTRY

2 cups flour (presifted)	3 to 4 tablespoons cold water
1 teaspoon salt	
¾ cup vegetable shortening	

Measure flour and salt into a bowl. Cut in shortening until well mixed. Sprinkle cold water over mixture and stir with a fork just until it holds together. Lightly flour a board or pastry cloth, halve the pastry and roll out lightly. Press pastry into two 9-inch pie plates. Crimp the edges. Prick each shell with fork. Bake at 400° for 30 minutes or until golden brown.

Enough for 2 single crusts.

MILLIE NELSON
Goffstown, New Hampshire

Millie and Ed Nelson designed and built their house in Goffstown, New Hampshire, when they were both in their sixties. There is a distinctly Oriental feeling about the furnishings and the arrangement of space, and it's no wonder, for the Nelsons spent many years in China as missionaries and teachers in the 1940s and 1950s.

"The Chinese have a marvelous way of cooking," says Millie, "and we can learn a lot from it. For instance, their recipes stretch meat very far, and they supplement the protein with tofu (soybean curd). A half pound of meat, shredded and added to vegetables and sauce, can easily feed four people."

Millie sometimes seasons vegetables with dill, basil, or fresh anise greens. Ginger root is also used to flavor some of her dishes. She buys a large root (it is readily available in most markets) and keeps it in a plastic bag in the freezer, breaking off a small chunk when needed and grating it while it's still frozen.

Millie's cooking is a happy marriage of her exposure to Chinese culture and her life in New England, tempered with an inheritance from Swedish ancestors. Consequently, dinner at the Nelsons' looks and tastes like an international feast fit for royalty.

ASSORTED VEGETABLES DISH

"The Chinese technique for cooking vegetables is fast, doesn't waste nutrients, and preserves their flavor and color. Americans spoil vegetables by cooking them in a lot of water and then throwing the water away."

3 tablespoons cooking oil
2 cups shredded Chinese cabbage
½ cup sliced mushrooms
½ cup finely sliced bamboo shoots (use canned shoots, drained)
½ green pepper, cut into thin strips
1 cup chicken broth
1 scant teaspoon salt
½ teaspoon sugar
1 tablespoon cornstarch dissolved in 3 tablespoons water

Heat oil. When very hot, add cabbage, mushrooms, bamboo shoots, and green pepper. Stir-fry for 2 to 3 minutes. Add broth, salt, and sugar, and cook for 3 to 4 minutes. Stir in cornstarch and water mixture. As soon as sauce is slightly thick, serve with steamed rice. *Serves 4.*

STIR-FRIED SNOW PEAS

Millie marinates the chicken in egg white for an hour to help keep the meat juicy when it is cooked. Sometimes she substitutes tofu for the chicken, browning it in a wok.

1 chicken breast, boned and skinned, cut into very thin strips
1 egg white
3 to 4 tablespoons cooking oil
½ pound fresh snow peas or sugar snap peas, stemmed
1 cup sliced fresh mushrooms
½ teaspoon sugar
½ teaspoon salt
1 tablespoon cooking wine
1½ cups chicken broth
1 tablespoon cornstarch

Marinate chicken slivers in egg white for 1 hour. Heat oil hot (375° in an electric wok or skillet) and quickly stir-fry chicken slivers about 2 minutes. Lift out of oil into a dish and cover. If necessary add another tablespoon of oil and heat the skillet again. Put in the snow peas and mushrooms, and stir-fry 3 to 4 minutes, then add sugar, salt, wine, and 1 cup of the broth. Bring to a boil and add cornstarch dissolved in remaining ½ cup broth. Boil again, add chicken, and serve.   *Serves 4-6.*

FISH WITH SWEET-SOUR SAUCE

Millie's cooking is famous among her neighbors, and what they most often request is Chinese food. The sweet-sour sauce in this dish would also go well with chicken or pork, prepared the same way as the fish — dipped in batter and deep-fried.

1 pound sole, flounder, or haddock fillets	1 egg
1 tablespoon each, cooking sherry and vinegar	½ cup water
	½ teaspoon salt
	1 quart cooking oil
¾ cup flour	Sweet-Sour Sauce (recipe follows)

Cut fish into 1½-inch pieces. Marinate in sherry and vinegar for 2 hours. Make a batter of the flour, egg, water, and salt. Drain fish and dip pieces into the batter. Fry in hot oil until golden brown. Serve with Sweet-Sour Sauce. *Serves 4.*

SWEET-SOUR SAUCE

3 stalks green onions, chopped	4 to 5 tablespoons brown sugar
½ green pepper, chopped	1 cup water
2 tablespoons corn oil	1½ tablespoons cornstarch
3 thin slices fresh ginger root (if available)	Small amount of cold water
1 tablespoon soy sauce	2 tablespoons vinegar

Sauté chopped onions and green pepper in the oil. Add ginger root, soy sauce, brown sugar, and 1 cup water. Boil for 1 or 2 minutes. Dissolve cornstarch in a small amount of cold water, and use it to thicken the sauce. Add the vinegar, then pour sauce over hot deep-fried fish and serve. *Makes about 1¼ cups.*

MEAT-VEGETABLE DUMPLINGS
(Wontons, or Chinese Chiao Tze)

Millie's famous wontons are similar to the boiled wontons you get in soup at Chinese restaurants, but hers are deep-fried and infinitely more delectable. She usually uses a non-hydrogenated corn oil for frying, although other kinds of oil, such as peanut, sesame, or safflower, are fine. She saves and reuses the oil, boiling a couple of slices of raw potato in it to remove strong flavors.

1 pound ground beef
½ pound Chinese cabbage or spinach, minced
3 green onions including stems, or 1 small onion, minced
1 tablespoon minced fresh ginger root, or ½ teaspoon ground
1 tablespoon sherry or cooking wine
3 tablespoons soy sauce
2 tablespoons cooking oil
1 teaspoon salt
1 teaspoon sugar
2 tablespoons cornstarch
1 package egg-roll wrappers
Oil for deep-frying

Combine all but last two ingredients and mix well. Stir for 5 to 10 minutes. Set aside in refrigerator for an hour. Take 1 package of wrappings — usually called egg-roll wrappers or spring-roll casings — and cut each casing into 4 squares, each about 3 to 4 inches on a side. Place about 1 teaspoon of the filling in the center of the wrapper, moisten around the edges, and fold over to seal meat inside. Heat oil to 375° and cook 6 to 8 wontons at a time for 4 to 5 minutes. Be careful not to crowd them or add too many, which would lower the temperature of the oil too much. Refrigerate the filled wrappers if you must wait a while before cooking them.

Serves 6.

(Cont'd)

215

Variations: These dumplings may be boiled in broth, if desired, for about 10 minutes. If boiled, you may wish to use half ground pork and half ground beef in the filling. For added flavor, you may add 5 or 6 chopped water chestnuts or several chopped mushrooms to the filling.

SHREDDED VEGETABLES AND BEEF

Lean pork or chicken may be substituted for the beef, but should be cooked slightly longer. Peas, green beans, broccoli, or other vegetables may be substituted for the carrots and turnips. Peas will need only two minutes to cook.

½ pound beef, cut into shreds	3 medium carrots
2 tablespoons cooking sherry	3 white turnips
2 tablespoons soy sauce	5 green onion stalks, or 1 medium onion
1 egg white	1 tablespoon corn oil
3 tablespoons corn oil	½ cup water
2 teaspoons cornstarch	½ teaspoon salt
	1 teaspoon sugar

Marinate beef in sherry, soy sauce, and egg white for about 2 hours. Heat corn oil in skillet. When very hot, quickly stir cornstarch into drained meat and put it into the hot oil. Fry only about 2 minutes and remove from skillet. Shred the carrots and turnips. Cut the onions into small pieces. Place 1 tablespoon corn oil in the skillet and heat. Put the vegetables into the oil and stir them well. Then add water and simmer for about 7 minutes. Add salt and sugar. Mix the beef with the vegetables and serve. *Serves 4.*

LION'S HEAD MEATBALLS

Great tasting and fun to eat, these large meatballs really do look like lions' heads with cabbage manes. The amount of salt called for can be reduced or omitted entirely.

1½ pounds ground pork and beef (equal amounts of each)
2 to 3 tablespoons soy sauce
2 tablespoons dry sherry
½ teaspoon salt
2 tablespoons cornstarch
3 tablespoons minced onion
1 teaspoon minced ginger root
6 water chestnuts, minced
½ cup cold water

Place all ingredients except water in large bowl. Mix well, then gradually add the water, stirring vigorously for 8 to 10 minutes. Set aside.

1 medium-size Chinese or savoy cabbage
3 tablespoons cooking oil
3 tablespoons cornstarch
⅓ cup water
4 tablespoons soy sauce
1 teaspoon sugar

Separate cabbage leaves and cut into 2-inch pieces. Heat oil in skillet or wok until hot and sauté or stir-fry cabbage for 2 minutes. Place cabbage in a stove-top casserole or cooking pot. Make 6 or 7 large meatballs from the meat mixture (above). Dissolve the cornstarch in the water and coat each meatball with the solution, then place meatballs on top of cabbage. Mix the soy sauce and sugar and pour over the meatballs and cabbage. Steam slowly for 30 to 40 minutes. Serve with steamed rice.

Serves 6.

SWEDISH CARDAMOM COFFEE BREAD

For her baking, Millie prefers to use King Arthur or another unbleached white flour, and she stirs her bread dough in one direction only. "Clockwise seems most natural to me, but the other way would work, too. I think it breaks down the gluten too much if you stir in too many directions. When most of the flour is in, I begin to stir in a circle from top to bottom, turning the bowl as I go." This rich, spicy bread makes a nice gift. Keep extra loaves on hand in the freezer.

2 tablespoons dry yeast	1 teaspoon powdered
⅓ cup warm water	cardamom, or more
2½ cups milk	to taste (or crush 12
1 cup sugar	pods)
1½ teaspoons salt	3 eggs, beaten slightly
8 to 9 cups flour	Sugar and cinnamon
1 cup butter, melted	

Dissolve yeast in warm water. Heat milk to warm. Add yeast, sugar, and salt to warm milk. Then gradually stir in 4 cups of flour and stir the batter with a spoon using 100 strokes or more, stirring in 1 direction only. Add the cooled melted butter, the cardamom, and the eggs. Stir well. Gradually add the remaining flour, 1 cup at a time, until 4 more cups have been worked into the dough. If needed, add up to a cup more flour. Knead dough until smooth. Cover with a cloth and let rise to double. Punch down and let rest on floured board about 10 minutes. Divide into 4 pieces. Cut each piece into 3 strips and make a braid. Place each braid in a greased baking pan and let rise until double. Brush tops with slightly beaten egg, and sprinkle with sugar and cinnamon. Bake at 375° about 20 minutes. Tap lightly with fingers to see if they are done (they will sound hollow). *Makes 4 loaves.*

RYE BREAD

A flavorful, chewy bread that can be glamorized with grated orange peel, caraway seeds, fennel, or candied citron peel at Christmastime. Millie doesn't let her breads rise too much before baking because it makes the texture too crumbly, and she cools most breads on their sides to help them keep their shape.

⅔ cup molasses
½ cup butter or
 margarine, melted
1 tablespoon salt
2 tablespoons dry
 yeast, dissolved in ⅓
 cup warm water

1 quart milk, heated to
 about 100°
7 cups rye flour
3 to 4 cups white flour
Butter

Add molasses, melted butter, salt, and yeast to warmed milk. Stir in rye flour, 2 cups at a time. Continue stirring until very smooth, always in one direction. Then add the white flour, again stirring or kneading until smooth. Let rise until double in bulk. Punch down and let rise again. Knead on floured board, add more flour if dough is sticky. Shape into 4 or 5 loaves to fit your pans — oblong or round pans are good. Let rise until almost double in bulk. Bake in 350° oven until done. Butter the tops when you take them out of the oven.

Makes 4-5 loaves.

DINNER ROLLS

"These rolls are my own recipe, and I've been making them for years. I must have given away thousands of them. The recipe makes about nine dozen, but you can make fewer rolls and use the rest of the dough for bread if you prefer. The rolls also freeze well after they're baked."

2 tablespoons dry yeast
½ cup warm water
5 cups milk
1 cup sugar
1 tablespoon salt
13 cups flour
   (approximately)

2 eggs, slightly beaten
1 cup shortening,
   melted
Butter, softened

Dissolve yeast in warm water. Heat milk to warm — about 100°. Add sugar, salt, and yeast to milk. Gradually stir in 7 cups of flour, and, using a spoon, stir the batter an additional 100 to 150 strokes. Add the beaten eggs and melted shortening. Stir well, then add the remaining flour, 1 cup at a time, until about 6 cups have been added. When stirring, use a wooden spoon, and stir in 1 direction only. Cover with a damp cloth and let rise until double in bulk. Punch down and let rest on floured board for 10 minutes.

Take about ¼ of the dough and roll out the piece to ¼-inch thickness. Spread it with soft butter. Cut wedges to desired size, roll them up, and place them on an oiled cookie sheet to rise, about 36 rolls to a sheet. When the rolls have doubled, bake at 400° until lightly browned. *Makes 8-10 dozen rolls.*

BRYSELL COOKIES

Brysell is the Swedish spelling for Brussels. These cookies are similar in taste to sugar cookies and are nice for packing in a lunch or serving at tea time.

2 cups butter
1 cup confectioners
  sugar

3 cups flour
1 teaspoon vanilla

Cream butter and sugar, and add flour and vanilla. Shape into logs and roll in colored sugar, crushed nuts, or pearl sugar. Chill at least 2 hours. Slice into ¼-inch rounds. Bake at 350° for 7 to 9 minutes on ungreased baking sheet. *Makes 4 dozen.*

RHUBARB PUDDING

This makes a fine dessert or tasty accompaniment to roast beef.

6 slices white bread
4 cups diced rhubarb
1½ cups brown and
  granulated sugar (¾
  cup each), or
  substitute 1 cup
  maple syrup or
  honey

Cinnamon
Nutmeg
1½ cups hot milk
4 eggs

Layer 2 slices bread, half the rhubarb, and half the sweetening into a greased casserole. Sprinkle with cinnamon and nutmeg. Repeat, ending with bread on top. Pour hot milk over all. Beat 4 eggs slightly and pour over top. Bake 1 hour at 350.

Serves 6.

SHIRLEY OLADELL
Litchfield, Connecticut

Shirley Oladell is the kind of cook who can take a familiar dish like bread pudding or chicken salad and make it with such care, special touches, and visual appeal that eating it is like going home to the kind of food you remember your mother making. From girlhood on she has been cooking and baking for family, friends, and community groups, and as a result has learned shortcuts and developed new techniques all along the way. "When I'm developing a new recipe," she says, "I try to figure out what tastes go together. The Sweet Potato and Pineapple Casserole is my own recipe. I decided to combine the sweetness of the potatoes with the tartness of the pineapple, and it seemed to me that honey would taste a little better in it than brown sugar."

Shirley prefers using butter for shortening in muffins. "My rule is that 'Butter tastes better in batter.' In casseroles or other dishes where the butter taste is not as important, I use margarine to save money. I think every cook is conscious of high prices these days. I don't like to waste anything — I add even small amounts of leftover vegetables to a plastic bag in my freezer for later use in soups."

223

TWO-CABBAGE SLAW

The colorful combination of red and green cabbage, plus the piquant flavor of horseradish makes this an exceptional salad.

½ head green cabbage
½ head red cabbage
½ cup mayonnaise
2 tablespoons lemon juice
2 tablespoons cider vinegar
2 tablespoons salad oil
2 tablespoons sugar
2 tablespoons horseradish
1 teaspoon salt
1 teaspoon celery seed
¼ teaspoon black pepper

Shred cabbages thinly. Place in large bowl. In a quart jar, combine remaining ingredients and shake well. Pour over cabbage and toss to mix well. Cover bowl and let stand several hours so the flavors will blend. *Serves 6.*

CORN PUDDING

If using fresh corn, you might want to reduce or omit the sugar altogether; however, canned corn is greatly improved by the addition.

2 cups whole corn (fresh or canned)
2 tablespoons flour
2 tablespoons sugar
3 tablespoons butter
1 teaspoon salt
3 eggs
1¾ cups milk

Combine corn, flour, sugar, butter, and salt in blender and mix well. Add eggs, one at a time, mixing after each egg. Add milk and blend until well mixed. Pour into a greased 1½-quart casserole and bake at 325° for about 1 hour, or until set, stirring once after 20 minutes. *Serves 6.*

CARROT CASSEROLE

Instead of chopped onion, Shirley recommends using it grated, which imparts the desired flavor but omits the chunks that are unappealing to some palates.

1 pound carrots	½ teaspoon salt
¼ cup carrot liquid (see directions)	½ teaspoon black pepper
2 tablespoons grated onion	½ cup seasoned bread crumbs, or packaged
¾ teaspoon horseradish	stuffing mix
½ cup mayonnaise	¼ cup butter, melted

Scrape carrots and cut on diagonal, making slices about ¼-inch thick. Cook in salted water until tender but still crisp. Drain, reserving ¼ cup cooking liquid. Mix onion, horseradish, mayonnaise, salt, pepper, and carrot liquid; combine with carrots in a buttered casserole. Mix the bread crumbs with the melted butter and spread over the carrots. Bake at 375° for 15 to 20 minutes or until bubbly.   *Serves 6.*

SWEET POTATO AND PINEAPPLE CASSEROLE

A very sweet dish that goes well with pork or fowl.

6 small sweet potatoes
1 small can crushed
  pineapple, drained
Dash of salt

½ cup miniature
  marshmallows
⅓ cup honey

Boil potatoes with skins on. When cool enough to handle, peel and slice into ½-inch pieces. Layer sweet potatoes and pineapple in a buttered 1-quart casserole. Add dash of salt. Top with marshmallows and pour honey over all. Bake for 10 minutes at 400°.

Serves 6-8.

HOT CHICKEN SALAD

Celery, nuts, and bread cubes give this an appealing texture.

2 cups cubed, cooked
  chicken
1½ cups thinly sliced
  celery
1 cup mayonnaise
½ cup toasted, slivered
  almonds
2 teaspoons lemon juice

2 teaspoons grated
  onion
½ teaspoon salt
1 cup toasted bread
  cubes
⅓ to ½ cup grated
  Parmesan cheese

Combine all ingredients except bread cubes and cheese in large bowl. Toss lightly until mixed well. Spoon into a baking dish without packing ingredients down. Sprinkle bread cubes over mixture and then sprinkle with grated cheese. Bake at 400° for 15 minutes or until bubbly. Serve with your favorite tossed salad.

Serves 6.

SKILLET CHICKEN TETRAZZINI

Chicken and noodles blended with a smooth, creamy sauce, and enhanced by the rosemary and Parmesan cheese topping.

3-pound chicken	1 small onion, minced
2½ cups water	¼ cup flour
¼ teaspoon black pepper	¼ teaspoon rosemary
3 teaspoons salt	¼ teaspoon paprika
8 ounces noodles	½ cup half-and-half cream
5 tablespoons butter or margarine	1 tablespoon grated Parmesan cheese

Place chicken breast-side down in large pot. Add water, pepper, and 2 teaspoons salt. Over high heat bring to boil. Reduce heat to low, cover pot, and simmer 35 minutes. Remove chicken to large bowl; refrigerate 30 minutes. Meanwhile strain broth, reserving 2 cups. When chicken is cool, cut meat into bite-size pieces, and discard bones and skin. Set chicken aside. Prepare noodles as directed on box; drain. In large skillet over medium heat, melt 2 tablespoons butter or margarine, add onion, and cook until tender. Remove onions and melt remaining 3 tablespoons butter; stir in flour, rosemary, the remaining 1 teaspoon salt, and paprika. Gradually add chicken broth and cook, stirring constantly, until thick. Stir in cream, chicken, noodles, and onion, and cook over low heat until mixture is heated through. Sprinkle with Parmesan cheese and additional paprika. *Serves 6.*

REFRIGERATOR BRAN MUFFINS

You can have fresh muffins every morning with this bran batter on hand in the refrigerator.

2 cups boiling water	4 eggs
6 cups All-Bran cereal	1 quart buttermilk
1 cup raisins	6 cups flour
2 cups sugar	5 teaspoons baking soda
½ cup honey	2 teaspoons salt
1 cup plus 3 tablespoons shortening	

Pour boiling water over 2 cups of bran cereal; add raisins, stir, and set aside. In large bowl, cream sugar, honey, and shortening. Add eggs and beat well. Blend in buttermilk. Add to bran and raisin mixture. Add the remaining 4 cups bran and mix. Sift flour with soda and salt. Add to bran mixture and mix well. Cover tightly and store in refrigerator. This will keep for 6 weeks. To bake muffins, merely spoon into greased muffin tins *without stirring,* filling tins half full, and bake 20 to 30 minutes in a preheated 400° oven. *Makes about 3 dozen.*

PIONEER BREAD PUDDING

The hardest part of this simple dessert is waiting to eat it.

2 cups milk	Pinch of salt
3 tablespoons butter	½ teaspoon vanilla
¼ cup sugar	2 cups bread cubes
2 eggs	Ground nutmeg

Scald milk with butter and sugar. Beat eggs slightly and add salt. Gradually stir in the warm milk mixture and vanilla. Place bread cubes in a buttered casserole and pour the milk mixture

(Cont'd)

over the bread. Sprinkle with nutmeg. Set the baking dish in a pan of warm water up to the level of the pudding. Bake at 350° for 1 hour. *Serves 6.*

RICH STRAWBERRY SHORTCAKE

Shirley always uses her hands to shape the dough for strawberry shortcake. "The biscuits seem to come out lighter this way than by rolling because you don't have to use extra flour, which can toughen them." When whipping cream for the topping, she adds about a teaspoonful of unflavored gelatin to keep the cream from "weeping" after it is whipped and to help it hold its consistency.

2 cups flour	1 egg, beaten
2 tablespoons sugar	⅔ cup light cream
1 tablespoon baking	4 cups sliced
powder	strawberries,
½ teaspoon salt	sugared
½ cup butter or	1 cup whipping cream
margarine	

Sift flour, sugar, baking powder, and salt together; cut in butter until mixture looks like coarse crumbs. Combine egg and cream; add all at once to dry ingredients, stirring only enough to moisten flour mixture. Turn dough out on lightly floured board and knead gently for 30 seconds. Pat with hands to ½-inch thickness. Cut 6 biscuits with floured 2½-inch cutter. Bake on ungreased baking sheet at 450° for about 10 minutes. Split biscuits while still warm and spread with butter. Pile strawberries on bottom half; add top half and spoon whipped cream over shortcake. Place a whole berry in center of cream for garnish. *Serves 6.*

STRAWBERRY PIE PLATTER WITH ORANGE SAUCE

A lovely dessert for a party. Be sure to pick over the strawberries carefully, using only those that are ripe yet firm.

Pastry for single-crust
   pie
1 quart fresh
   strawberries, cleaned
   and hulled
2 tablespoons sugar
Orange Sauce (recipe
   follows)
Whipped cream

Roll pastry into a 10-inch circle. Place on pizza pan or cookie sheet and flute edge after folding in ½ inch. Prick pastry all over with a fork and bake at 400° for about 10 to 15 minutes or until lightly browned. Set aside to cool. Place strawberries, stem ends down, in circles on the crust. Brush with Orange Sauce and sprinkle with sugar. Cut pie into wedges and serve with Orange Sauce and whipped cream.

ORANGE SAUCE

1 cup sugar
¼ teaspoon salt
2 tablespoons
   cornstarch
1 cup orange juice
¼ cup lemon juice
¾ cup water

In small saucepan, mix sugar, salt, and cornstarch. Stir in juices and water. Cook, stirring constantly, until mixture boils and thickens. Boil 1 minute. Cool.

NOTES

DOROTHY OLIVEIRA
Rehoboth, Massachusetts

Dorothy Oliveira has been cooking for the
townspeople of Rehoboth for over thirty years — as cook at the
Palmer River Elementary School, as organizer of countless
fund-raising dinners, and as owner of a catering business. "My
grandmother taught me to cook," she says. "I was the oldest
of eight and started cooking when ten, so I learned to cook for
a lot of people right from the beginning."

Dorothy and her husband, Frank, raise their own corn,
tomatoes, peppers, muskmelons, squash, and strawberries,
with plenty left over to sell to local customers. During summer,
Dorothy fills two freezers with their produce. When freezing,
she says, the most important thing is to make sure both
vegetables and fruit are fresh-picked. She freezes all vegetables
raw and doesn't wash them unless they have been sprayed
within two weeks of picking. She double-bags them to ensure
freshness, and freezes strawberries, blueberries, and other fruit in
boxes so as not to crush the fruit.

She also insists on using fresh eggs, and her grandmother
taught her that the way to tell a fresh egg is to put it in a
bowl of water. If it rises to the top, the egg isn't fresh. "I take
the eggs out of the refrigerator at least an hour before I plan
to use them," she says. "Egg whites become stiff much sooner
when they're warm."

The Oliveiras are a close family, and each member has a
favorite dish, but the one they ask for most is Dorothy's
chicken fricassee, which has an interesting story behind it.
About fifteen years ago, her son Frank Jr. was living in

California and hadn't seen his parents in three years, so unbeknown to him his wife arranged for Dorothy to cook her chicken fricassee for the "Truth or Consequences" TV show, which flew Dorothy and Frank Sr. out at the show's expense. On the show, while Dorothy was hidden, her son was asked to try three different chicken fricassees, all made according to his mother's recipe. He did so, and stopped at the dish which Dorothy had brought with her. "Nobody," he said, "but my mother makes chicken fricassee like this."

CHICKEN FRICASSEE

Dorothy's family insists that she make this for Christmas dinner; it's their all-time favorite. Chourico, a spicy Portuguese sausage, and Assafroa, Portuguese paprika, are available in Portuguese communities and in some of the larger supermarkets throughout New England.

5-pound fowl or
  roasting chicken, cut
  in pieces
1½ teaspoons allspice
3 teaspoons salt
1 large onion, diced
Water to cover
2 whole chourico
  (Portuguese sausage)

2 cups raw rice, washed
  and soaked for 1
  hour in *cold* water to
  cover
1 teaspoon Assafroa
  (Portuguese paprika)
1 teaspoon allspice
1 teaspoon salt

Place chicken, 1½ teaspoons allspice, 3 teaspoons salt, and onion in large pot and add enough water to cover. Simmer for 1½ hours. Prick the chourico (to release more flavor), add to stewing chicken, and continue simmering. Bring rice and soaking water to a simmer, uncovered; add Assafroa, 1 teaspoon allspice, and 1 teaspoon salt, and cook uncovered for

(Cont'd)

20 to 25 minutes, or until tender. Do not stir rice (or it will become sticky). If more liquid is needed while the rice cooks, ladle in some broth from the chicken pot and replace what was removed from there with water. When the rice is done, transfer it to a large serving dish, arrange the chicken and chourico on top, and serve. *Serves 8-10.*

OLD-FASHIONED DROP COOKIES

These taste like gingerbread. Great for snacks or with a dish of coffee ice cream.

1 cup sugar	1 teaspoon ginger
½ cup shortening	1 teaspoon baking
1 egg	soda
3 to 3½ cups flour	½ teaspoon salt
(batter should be	½ cup molasses
neither thin nor stiff)	½ cup water
1 teaspoon cinnamon	

Cream sugar and shortening. Add egg. In a separate bowl, mix flour, cinnamon, ginger, soda, and salt. Combine molasses and water, and add alternately with dry ingredients to shortening mixture. Drop by spoonfuls on cookie sheet. Bake at 350° for 10 minutes. *Makes about 5½ dozen.*

BLUEBERRY SLUMP

So simple, so good. Use fresh or dry-frozen berries.

1 quart blueberries	Baking Powder
1 cup sugar	Dumplings (recipe
¼ teaspoon nutmeg	follows)

Wash and clean blueberries. Add sugar and nutmeg. Cover with water and let come to rolling boil. Reduce heat, add dumplings, cover, and simmer for 15 minutes. Serve hot.

Serves 6-8.

Baking Powder Dumplings:

2 cups flour	2 tablespoons
2 teaspoons baking	shortening
powder	½ cup milk
¼ teaspoon salt	

Mix all ingredients together and drop into blueberry mixture.

INDIAN PUDDING

A New England favorite. Serve warm with cream, or with vanilla or coffee ice cream.

3 cups milk	½ teaspoon ginger
¼ cup molasses	½ teaspoon cinnamon
3 tablespoons	½ cup cold milk
cornmeal	Lump of butter the
1 egg	size of an egg (about
½ cup sugar	½ stick butter)
½ teaspoon salt	

Scald 3 cups milk, add molasses and cornmeal, and cook until thick. Remove from heat. Blend together egg, sugar, salt, ginger, and cinnamon; add to milk mixture. Pour into greased

(Cont'd)

1-quart casserole. Bake for 30 minutes at 325°; add ½ cup *cold* milk and butter. Continue baking for about 1 hour.

Serves 6.

POMPADOUR PUDDING

Dorothy's grandchildren love this old-fashioned pudding. It can be made in a flash, but should be thoroughly chilled, for an hour or more, before serving.

1 quart milk
4 tablespoons
   cornstarch
½ cup sugar
¼ teaspoon salt
1 teaspoon vanilla
2 egg yolks, slightly
   beaten

4 squares unsweetened
   chocolate
4 tablespoons milk
¾ cup confectioners
   sugar
2 egg whites

Scald 1 quart milk. Mix cornstarch, sugar, salt, vanilla, and egg yolks; add to milk and cook until thick. Pour mixture into 1- or 1½-quart casserole. Melt chocolate, and add the 4 tablespoons milk, and confectioners sugar. Whip egg whites stiff and fold into melted chocolate. Spread chocolate mixture on top of custard mixture. Bake at 350° for 10 to 15 minutes. Chocolate mixture will puff up when done.   *Serves 6-8.*

Dorothy Rathbun
Saunderstown, Rhode Island

Dorothy Rathbun's cookbook consists of loose sheets of paper and other handwritten pages pasted onto the days of a one-year diary. The recipes are gifts from friends or pieces of the past out of Dorothy's mother's kitchen in the Annapolis Valley of Nova Scotia. But some of Dorothy's best-known dishes are from recipes she prepares from memory — like her peanut butter fudge, jonny cakes, a variety of breads, and clam chowder.

Dorothy has made her chowder for years now for the annual Wickford (Rhode Island) Art Festival, and it is so popular that it brings people back to the event year after year. "Some people tell us they've come every year since the beginning and they only come for the food. If it was the art, they wouldn't even come to the festival, but they seem to like chowder."

WICKFORD CLAM CHOWDER

"Some people don't like evaporated milk, but I think it gives the chowder a little something extra. Plain milk chowder tastes like bellywash to me."

5 pounds potatoes, peeled and diced	1 can (13 ounces) evaporated milk
1 quart quahogs, chopped	1 quart whole milk, warmed
1 pint quahog juice	Celery salt
⅓ cup cut up salt pork	Paprika
½ cup chopped onion	Salt and pepper to taste

Cook potatoes in enough water to cover, until done. Mash the potatoes slightly to make the chowder creamier. Add the quahogs and juice, and cook the mixture slowly. In a skillet, fry the salt pork, then scoop out most of the scraps from the fat. ("Pork scraps floating in clam chowder aren't attractive to some people.") Cook the chopped onion in the fat until soft. Add the onion to the quahogs and potatoes, and bring to a boil. Remove from heat and add evaporated milk slowly. Then add whole milk (slightly heated to avoid curdling). Add celery salt, paprika, and salt and pepper. Take care not to boil the chowder once the milk is added, and do not cover the pot while the chowder is warm or it will curdle.   *Serves 20.*

JONNY CAKES

Rhode Island jonny cakes are usually served in restaurants with syrup, but the Rathbuns like them with gravy, and Dorothy often prepares a meal of creamed chipped beef, baked potatoes, carrots, and jonny cakes. She uses Kenyon's Jonny Cake meal, which is available from the Kenyon Corn Meal Company, Usquepaugh, West Kingston, RI 02892.

                                                        (Cont'd)

1 cup Kenyon's Jonny Cake meal	1 teaspoon sugar
½ teaspoon salt	Boiling water
	Milk

Combine meal, salt, and sugar, and pour boiling water over mixture very slowly, just enough to swell the meal. Let sit for a few minutes. Add enough milk so that the mixture will drop from a spoon onto a hot griddle. This makes a thick griddle cake. Turn to brown other side and serve hot. *Makes about 8.*

MOIST OATMEAL BREAD

An exceptional bread. For variety, use up to three cups whole wheat flour and the rest white. Dorothy uses King Arthur flour in her baking, and when she goes to Canada, she always comes home with a twenty-pound bag of Canadian flour. "Somehow, it seems to swell up much more than our flours do. And sometimes I buy Robin Hood flour, which is Canadian and available in A&P stores here."

2 cups oatmeal	¾ cup molasses (or a
1 tablespoon salt	mixture of molasses
1 tablespoon lard	and honey)
4 cups boiling water	11 cups flour, or
1 yeast cake, dissolved in 1 cup lukewarm water	enough to make a dough you can knead

Combine first 4 ingredients and set aside to cool. Stir in yeast and molasses. Gradually add flour and knead until smooth and elastic. Cover, let rise until double in volume, punch down, and divide dough among 4 small bread pans. Let rise again, covered, until double in volume, then bake at 375° for 15 minutes; reduce heat to 325° and bake 30 minutes longer, or until bread tests done. *Makes 4 loaves.*

WHITE BREAD

A firm, chewy white bread — great for hearty sandwiches, for croutons, or as a canapé base. The finished loaves are a lovely golden brown, with high, straight sides.

4 cups lukewarm
water
⅓ cup shortening,
melted (chicken fat,
bacon fat,
margarine, or lard)
⅓ cup sugar
1 cake or 1 tablespoon
dry yeast, softened
in ½ cup lukewarm
water

1 tablespoon salt
12 cups flour, or
enough to make a
dough you can
knead

Combine ingredients and knead the dough until it is smooth and elastic. Allow to rise until double in volume (about 1 hour, 45 minutes), then punch down, divide into quarters, and place in 4 greased 9x5-inch loaf pans. Allow dough to rise again until double in volume (about 1 hour). Put into a 400° oven for 15 minutes to "puff" the bread, then reduce to 325° for about 45 minutes. *Makes 4 loaves.*

MOLASSES WHOLE WHEAT BREAD

A slightly sweet bread, especially good toasted.

1 cup milk, scalded
⅓ cup molasses
1½ teaspoons salt
3 tablespoons
shortening, melted
1 yeast cake, dissolved
in ¼ cup lukewarm
water

1 egg, beaten
2 cups unsifted whole
wheat flour
2 to 2½ cups white
flour
Salad oil

(Cont'd)

Combine first 4 ingredients in large bowl. Cool to lukewarm Add yeast and egg, stir in flour, and knead until smooth. E with salad oil, cover, and let rise until double in volume. Punch down, shape into 4 buns, and place 2 buns each in 2 loaf pans. Brush tops with salad oil and let rise, covered, until doubled. Bake at 350° for 30 to 40 minutes, or until bread tests done. Cool in pans for 10 minutes; remove loaves from pans and return bread to oven for 5 to 10 minutes if necessary to dry out sides and bottom. *Makes 2 loaves.*

PEANUT BUTTER FUDGE

Another treat at the Wickford Art Festival is Dorothy's peanut butter fudge, which is lighter than most and has a pleasant texture.

2 cups sugar
½ cup milk
2 tablespoons butter
  or margarine
3 generous tablespoons
  Marshmallow Fluff

3 generous tablespoons
  peanut butter
1 teaspoon vanilla

Bring sugar, milk, and butter to a boil, and let boil for 3 minutes. Then add Marshmallow Fluff, peanut butter, and vanilla. Beat with a spoon — for only a few minutes — and pour into a greased square pan to set.

Makes about 3-4 dozen squares.

NELLIE REED
Owls Head, Maine

For years the people of Owls Head, Maine, have said that the best pie crust they have ever eaten is made by Nellie Reed. Then they add that the best filling between two crusts on the entire coast of Maine is Nellie's chicken pie. Her pies raised nearly $15,000 to start the fire department, and they have also benefited churches and civic organizations.

"The first time we put on a chicken pie supper for the fire department we made 100 pies, thinking that would be plenty. After that we always had to make at least 200. Each pie serves five people . . . . I like to go outside and see how many people are waiting. They ask, 'Is there enough chicken?' I say, 'I guess so, but if not, we have beans.' Oh, they don't like that. Some people buy two dinners just to have another piece of pie. We never worry about leftover pie. They barter for what's left." Nellie says she has lost count of how many chicken pies she has baked, but "it must be at least 3,000."

CHICKEN PIE

"My father never allowed us to have spices. In my chicken pie there are no spices, only the salt in the water that the chicken stews in."

3-pound roasting
    chicken, giblets
    removed
2 teaspoons salt
Water
1 can onion soup
Flour dissolved in
    water

1 teaspoon
    Gravymaster
    (optional)
Pastry for double-crust
    pie (recipe follows)
2 tablespoons butter

Stew chicken in salt and water to cover for about 1½ hours. When done, pull meat off bones and cut into bite-sized chunks. Refrigerate until following day.

Skim most of the fat off top of the chicken broth, leaving just enough for flavor. Add soup to broth and bring to a boil. Thicken with a paste made from flour and water, using as much as necessary for desired consistency. Add Gravymaster for coloring if desired. Strain gravy to remove onions. Put bottom crust in pie plate, fill with chicken, and cover with 1¾ cups gravy. Cover with top crust, spread with butter, and bake at 400° for 30 minutes. Serve hot with extra gravy.

Serves 6.

PIE CRUST

"The pie crust recipe I use is my mother's. It's as easy as rolling off a log. The secrets are using lard for flavor and plenty of water. Most pie crust is like cardboard because the dough lacked water."

1 pound lard
1 tablespoon salt

5¼ cups flour
1 cup water

(Cont'd)

Soften lard until it is pliable and put in mixing bowl. Add 1 tablespoon salt and the flour, and mix thoroughly with your hands until mixture is like soft putty. Add water and mix well. Section off dough for 4 double crusts. Freeze 3 sections in separate plastic bags. Roll dough thin for 1 double-crust pie.

Enough for 4 double-crust pies.

BAKED STUFFED HADDOCK

"When I cooked at the inn, this was my specialty. My family likes a wet stuffing, so that's how I make it." The baking time depends on the size of the fish used.

1 fresh whole haddock, scaled, with skin on	1 small onion
	½ teaspoon salt
	Black pepper to taste
4 slices butter	½ cup butter, melted
4 medium potatoes, boiled	1 egg, beaten
3 slices bread	Poultry seasoning to taste

Cut haddock crosswise 4 times. Place butter in each slit. Grind together potatoes, bread, and onion. Add salt, pepper, melted butter, and beaten egg. If dry, add milk. Add poultry seasoning to taste. Place stuffing under gills. Bake at 350°. Serve with favorite fish sauce.   *Quantity depends on size of fish.*

247

SEAFOOD CASSEROLE

Looks as extravagantly wonderful as it tastes! To make it less expensive, substitute haddock for lobster.

1 pound fillet of haddock	1 can cream of mushroom soup
½ pound scallops, cut up	1½ cups white or red wine
Butter	1 tablespoon cornstarch for thickening
2 lobsters	
1 can shrimp	
1 can minced clams	Dash of paprika

Boil 1 pound fillet of haddock for 15 to 20 minutes, being careful to keep it whole. Sauté scallops in butter with dash of paprika. Boil 2 lobsters, 20 to 25 minutes, and pick meat off. Flake haddock. Put haddock, lobster, scallops, shrimp, and clams in dish and mix lightly. Heat mushroom soup, wine, and cornstarch dissolved in water. Pour sauce over fish. Bake at 350° for 1 hour. *Serves 8-10.*

MOLASSES COOKIES

"I always have a loaf pan filled with molasses cookie mixture in my refrigerator. Whenever I need a dozen, I just slice them off the loaf and bake them."

1 cup molasses	4 cups flour
½ pound butter or margarine	2 teaspoons salt
1 cup sugar	1½ teaspoons ginger
2 teaspoons baking soda	½ teaspoon cloves
¼ cup hot water	½ teaspoon allspice
	2 teaspoons cinnamon

(Cont'd)

Bring molasses to boil. Remove from stove and melt butter in molasses. Place 1 cup sugar in mixing bowl. Add soda to hot water and dissolve. Add to molasses and pour over the sugar in bowl (molasses will froth over). Mix well. Sift flour, salt, and spices together. Add to molasses mixture and mix well. Put in loaf pan lined with waxed paper and refrigerate overnight. Cut dough thin. Bake at 325° for 12 to 15 minutes on well-greased cookie sheet. Remove from sheet immediately.

Makes 3-4 dozen.

MOLASSES-BLUEBERRY CAKE

"This is my grandmother's recipe. I think it's out of this world."

1 cup molasses
½ cup water
¼ teaspoon salt
  (optional)
2 tablespoons
  shortening

2 cups flour
1 teaspoon baking soda
2 cups blueberries

Mix all ingredients together in bowl. Bake at 350° in greased 8-inch square pan for 60 to 70 minutes, or until done.

Serves 6-8.

BARBARA RILEY
Cambridge, Massachusetts

Barbara Riley is not only a good cook, she's an artist who just happens to use a palette that is edible. She has a small catering business, and when she's not cooking for a party, she's cooking just for the love of it. "I spend my whole day in the kitchen — it's my research lab!" she says.

"I love to make things you'd never see in a restaurant. I make so many things now from scratch that I can skip whole aisles at the grocery store. It's time-consuming, of course, but I'm in the kitchen anyway, by choice. By making everything myself I can learn more about how ingredients interact. And it makes such a difference in the taste.

"When I make bread," says Barbara, "I look at a recipe, then go off and do my own thing." She prefers to make bread in small batches so that the dough is better kneaded. "Bread needs to grow. I make a sponge and let it stand, then go back and fool around with it. Sometimes I spend all day, off and on, with one batch of bread. Making a sponge first helps concentrate the flavors." Barbara uses a mixture of King Arthur or other high-gluten flour and all-purpose flour for most breads; for fancy yeast doughs she mixes cake and white flours. She also buys specialty flours and mixes them with the more conventional ones.

Barbara cooks for her family with the same care and flair that she applies to her catering, and consequently, the Rileys rarely eat out: "I don't look forward to it anymore," says Barbara. "My palate is so aware of things and I can't help criticizing the food. I criticize my own cooking that way, too."

HOMEMADE PEANUT BUTTER GRANOLA

A healthy breakfast cereal that gets the day off to a good start.

Boiling water
1 cup raisins
¾ cup creamy peanut butter or safflower butter
⅔ cup honey
1 teaspoon cinnamon
Dash of cloves

1 teaspoon vanilla
4 cups rolled oats
½ cup wheat germ
½ cup cut up dried figs or dates
1 cup shelled peanuts, sunflower seeds, or favorite unsalted nuts

Pour boiling water over raisins to cover and let stand for 10 minutes. Drain. In a saucepan, combine peanut or safflower butter, honey, cinnamon, and cloves, and heat through. Remove from heat and stir in vanilla. Place oats in a large shallow roasting pan and pour warm peanut butter mixture over the oats. Stir gently until mixture is coated, then spread evenly in the pan. Bake in a slow oven (300°) for 35 minutes, stirring occasionally. Turn off oven and stir in raisins, wheat germ, figs or dates, and nuts. Let granola dry in the oven for about 1½ hours, stirring occasionally. Store in covered containers. *Makes about 8 cups.*

STRAWBERRY-RHUBARB MUFFINS

Exceptional muffins with a tart-sweet flavor complemented by a cinnamon topping. Serve with Honey Butter, made by whipping half a cup of unsalted butter with two tablespoons honey and a tablespoon brandy.

1¾ cups all-purpose
   flour
½ cup granulated
   sugar
2½ teaspoons baking
   powder
Dash of salt
1 egg, lightly beaten
¾ cup milk
⅓ cup vegetable oil
1 teaspoon vanilla
¼ teaspoon cinnamon

1 tablespoon Grand
   Marnier (optional)
¾ cup minced fresh
   rhubarb
½ cup sliced
   strawberries
2 tablespoons brown
   sugar
¼ teaspoon cinnamon
6 small strawberries, cut
   in half

Mix flour, granulated sugar, baking powder, and salt in a large bowl. Combine egg, milk, oil, vanilla, and cinnamon (and Grand Marnier if desired) in a small bowl. Stir into flour mixture with fork until just moistened. Fold in rhubarb and strawberries. Fill well-buttered muffin tins two-thirds full. Combine brown sugar and cinnamon and sprinkle over batter; gently place a strawberry half on top of each muffin. Bake in a 400° oven until golden brown, about 20 to 25 minutes. Remove from tins and cool on wire racks. *Makes 12.*

CALCUTTA INDIAN BREAD

Barbara is adventurous in her cooking and especially enjoys experimenting with breads of all kinds, adding mustard, cheese, herbs, and minced vegetables from time to time.

1 envelope (1 scant tablespoon) dry yeast
1 tablespoon sugar
1 cup plus 2 tablespoons warm water
2 tablespoons unsalted butter
¼ cup minced shallots, or 2 garlic cloves, finely minced, combined with enough finely minced green onion to make ¼ cup

1 teaspoon mild curry powder
3 to 3½ cups flour (2 cups high-gluten flour and 1 to 1½ cups all-purpose flour)
1 teaspoon salt
½ teaspoon Dijon mustard
Cornmeal
1 egg
½ teaspoon salt

Combine yeast, sugar, and water, and let stand until yeast is foamy. Melt butter in a small skillet over low heat and add shallots or green onion and garlic mixture. Add a bit more butter if necessary, and stir in curry powder. Turn off heat and let mixture stand for 5 minutes. Combine 2½ cups flour, the curry mixture, 1 teaspoon salt, mustard, and the yeast mixture, and beat for 5 minutes. Cover bowl and let rest for half an hour.

Turn out dough on a floured work surface and knead in remaining flour to make a soft, pliable dough, adding more all-purpose flour if needed. Knead about 10 minutes. Place in oiled bowl and let rise, covered, until doubled; punch down and let rise again until doubled. Turn out dough on a floured work surface and divide dough in half. Roll out each half into

(Cont'd)

a rectangle and roll up into an oblong loaf, pinching ends and seam tightly. Place seam-side down on a cookie sheet sprinkled liberally with cornmeal. Cover loaves lightly with a damp cloth and let stand in a warm place until almost doubled — about 45 minutes.

Slash tops of loaves with a sharp knife or razor. Beat egg with ½ teaspoon salt and brush over loaves, being careful not to drip glaze onto pan. Bake in 425° oven until loaves are golden brown and sound hollow when tapped on the bottom — about 25 minutes. Cool on racks before slicing.

Makes 2 loaves.

MUSTARD À LA MAISON

A tasty addition to cream sauces and breads, or as a spread for sandwiches.

¼ cup dry mustard
  (Coleman's)
¼ cup dry white wine
  vinegar
⅓ cup dry white wine

1 tablespoon honey
½ teaspoon salt
2 dashes hot pepper
  sauce
3 egg yolks, beaten

Place the dry mustard, vinegar, wine, honey, salt, and pepper sauce in the top of a double boiler and stir together. Allow the mixture to stand for 2 hours so the flavors blend. Beat the egg yolks into the mustard mixture and cook over hot water, stirring constantly until slightly thickened (about 5 minutes). Pour into a jar, cool, and refrigerate until ready to use.

Makes 1 cup.

HOMEMADE CRACKERS

*A distinctive cheesy-mustardy taste — combined with the
nuttiness of the whole wheat — makes this a delightfully
different cracker. Roll out dough as thin as possible so crackers
will be real crisp. Serve with cocktails, dips, or spreads, and use
them, crushed, to top casseroles or to coat chicken pieces.*

1 cup grated sharp cheese	½ cup whole wheat flour (or enough to bind the dough)
1 stick butter	¼ cup milk
2 teaspoons Dijon mustard	Water
Cayenne pepper to taste	¼ to ½ cup sesame seeds (optional)
1½ cups unseasoned bread crumbs, preferably from homemade bread	

Mix together all ingredients except milk, water, and sesame
seeds, using a pastry cutter or fork. Add milk to make a
dough the consistency of pie crust. Freeze dough overnight. Cut
in half while still frozen, and after about half an hour roll out
and cut into desired cracker shapes. Place crackers on a greased
cookie sheet and prick with a fork. Brush lightly with water
and sprinkle with sesame seeds if desired. Bake at 350° for 8 to
10 minutes. Store in a covered container or in the freezer.
Warm briefly in the oven to crisp the crackers.

Makes about 4-5 dozen.

QUATRE ÉPICES (Four Spices)

Use this spice in pâtés, stews, meat loaves, and soups, and experiment with other dishes as well.

¾ cup ground white
    pepper
4 teaspoons ground
    cloves

4 teaspoons ground
    ginger
2 teaspoons ground
    nutmeg

Combine all ingredients until well blended, and store in tightly closed containers.　　　　　*Makes about 1 cup.*

ONION PIE

Quiche-like, with added tang and color from the tomatoes. Lovely for lunch or Sunday night supper.

3 tablespoons chicken
    fat or butter
4 onions, thinly sliced
¼ teaspoon thyme
3 eggs, beaten
¾ cup evaporated milk
¼ teaspoon nutmeg
2 dashes hot pepper
    sauce
½ teaspoon crushed
    caraway seed

½ teaspoon salt
9-inch pie shell,
    unbaked and chilled
1 egg white, slightly
    beaten
1 large beefsteak
    tomato, cut in thin
    slices
¾ cup mild Swiss
    cheese, shredded

Melt chicken fat or butter and cook onions with thyme over very low heat until transparent (about 20 minutes). Beat eggs, and add milk and seasonings. Brush pie crust with egg white. Fill crust with onions, tomato, and cheese, and spread the egg mixture over the top. Bake at 400° for 10 minutes; lower heat and bake an additional 20 minutes at 350°. Serve warm.

Serves 6.

LASAGNA ROLL-UPS

Beautiful blend of walnut and garlic flavors. Serve as an appetizer, side dish, or entrée.

Filling:

¾ pound lasagna, cooked al dente	½ cup whole-milk mozzarella cheese, grated
1 cup ricotta cheese	⅓ cup grated Parmesan cheese
1 egg yolk	¼ cup ground walnuts
½ teaspoon nutmeg	
Salt to taste	
2 drops hot pepper sauce, or cayenne pepper to taste	

Cook lasagna noodles until barely done. Combine remaining ingredients in a bowl and stir well.

Pesto Sauce:

2 tablespoons dried basil	2 garlic cloves
⅓ cup ground walnuts	Dash of salt
⅓ cup plus 1 tablespoon chopped fresh Italian parsley	1 cup olive oil
1 tablespoon minced green onion	⅓ cup plus 1 tablespoon grated Parmesan cheese

Combine all ingredients in a blender and mix until smooth.

To Assemble:

Spread 1 to 2 tablespoons of filling over each lasagna noodle. Roll up the lasagna end to end (jelly-roll style) and cut each roll-up in half, keeping jelly-roll style. Place cut-side down in

(Cont'd)

a greased baking dish. Spoon 1 to 2 teaspoons of pesto sauce over each roll-up. Cover tightly with buttered foil and bake at 300° for 20 minutes. *Serves 4-6.*

BANANA TART

A sinfully rich dessert of caramel, cream cheese, and rum-poached banana slices, topped with an apricot-rum glaze. Scrumptious!

- ½ cup granulated sugar
- ½ cup water
- ⅓ cup dark Jamaican rum
- 4 bananas, sliced into ½-inch pieces
- 1 package (8 ounces) cream cheese, softened
- ½ teaspoon vanilla
- ⅓ cup confectioners sugar
- ¼ teaspoon grated lemon rind
- 2 tablespoons sour cream
- ½ cup granulated sugar
- ½ stick butter
- 2 tablespoons heavy cream
- 8-inch pie shell or tart shell, baked
- ½ cup apricot jam
- 1 tablespoon rum

Bring ½ cup granulated sugar, water, and ⅓ cup rum to a boil, stirring and washing down any sugar crystals clinging to the sides of the pan with a brush dipped in cold water, and simmer for 5 minutes or until syrup forms. Poach the banana slices in batches in the syrup for only 3 minutes, and with a slotted spoon transfer to a dish to drain. Combine cream cheese, vanilla, confectioners sugar, lemon rind, and sour cream, and set aside. In a skillet over very low heat melt ½ cup granulated sugar, stirring constantly and being careful not to burn. Add butter and bring the mixture to a boil over low heat. Increase the heat to moderately high and cook, rotating the pan gently,

(Cont'd)

259

until it is a golden caramel. Remove the pan from the heat and stir in heavy cream. Spread the caramel over the pastry crust, tilting to cover, and let cool. Spread the cream cheese mixture over the caramel and arrange the bananas over the cream cheese. Melt apricot jam and rum over moderate heat. Bring to a boil and strain through a fine sieve into a bowl. Glaze the tart with the mixture while the glaze is still hot. Refrigerate until about 20 minutes before serving.   *Serves 8.*

NOTES

HELEN & BERTHA ROBB
West Brattleboro, Vermont

Although Bertha Robb and her daughter-in-law Helen are technically related only by marriage, their spirits are kindred, and they trade recipes and quips with the ease that comes from many years of friendship.

Since the sugarhouse on the Robb farm produces over 250 gallons of maple syrup each spring, the women never have to worry about running out. Instead, they have ample opportunity to experiment with creative new uses for maple syrup and sugar both. "Anything you use honey or molasses in, you can use maple syrup in, substituted in equal amounts," explains Helen. "If you substitute syrup for granulated sugar, you have to reduce the amount of liquid in the recipe."

Rather than using costly Grade A or Fancy in cooking, Bertha and Helen regularly use Grade B, a darker and even more flavorful syrup that is usually available to consumers from syrup producers at a much lower price than standard tourist-trade Grade A. "I would never choose Fancy for my household," says Bertha. "It's like champagne. You wouldn't want to have it all the time."

ROBB FARM FROSTY

Cool, light, and satisfying. Try this refreshing drink on a warm afternoon as a nutritious snack, or eliminate the ice cream and enjoy it for breakfast.

1 cup milk
1 scoop vanilla ice
   cream
1 egg

1 tablespoon maple
   syrup (or more to
   taste)

Put all ingredients into a blender and mix well. Serve in a tall glass.

Serves 1.

HELEN'S DOUGHNUTS

A good stick-to-the-ribs doughnut, frosted with maple cream. The spices can be increased, if a stronger flavor is desired.

4½ cups sifted flour
3½ teaspoons baking
   powder
1 teaspoon salt
½ teaspoon nutmeg
¼ teaspoon cinnamon

3 eggs
1 teaspoon vanilla
¾ cup sugar
3 tablespoons butter,
   softened
¾ cup milk

Sift dry ingredients together. Beat eggs, add vanilla and sugar, and beat well. Mix in butter. Alternately add milk and sifted ingredients to egg mixture to make a soft dough. Turn out on a floured board and knead lightly for about half a minute. Roll out to about ¼-inch thickness and cut with doughnut cutter. Fry in hot oil (375°) until golden brown. Drain and frost with maple cream.

Makes 12-16.

HELEN'S PANCAKES

*Lovely and light. If there are any leftover pancakes, freeze them,
as Helen does, after they are thoroughly cooled; reheat quickly in a
toaster oven.*

1 egg	1 tablespoon sugar
1¼ cups milk	1 tablespoon baking
¼ cup butter, melted	powder
1¼ cups flour	½ teaspoon salt

Beat together the egg, milk, and melted butter. In a separate
bowl, combine dry ingredients. Add liquid ingredients and stir
together until flour is moistened. Fry on seasoned griddle
(400°). Turn as the pancakes begin to bubble. Serve with warm
maple syrup. *Serves 4.*

MAPLE MOUNTAINS

*High, crusty, popover-like muffins that are elevated to the sublime
by being drenched in maple syrup. Serve while still warm.*

1 cup milk	½ teaspoon salt
1 scant cup flour	2 eggs
1 tablespoon melted	1 cup maple syrup
shortening, or oil	1 teaspoon butter

Combine first 4 ingredients and beat at high speed for 1
minute. Add eggs, one at a time, beating vigorously after each
addition. Fill greased custard cups two-thirds full and bake at
425° for 30 minutes. Remove from oven and drench with maple
syrup as follows: boil syrup gently with butter for 5 minutes.
(Watch pot to be sure syrup doesn't boil over.) Cool while
muffins bake and pour over tops when removed from oven. For
more saturation, pierce the muffins before pouring on the syrup.

Makes about 1 dozen.

MAPLE BRAN MUFFINS

One of the best-tasting muffins around, these will complement any meal and are destined to become a family favorite.

¾ cup maple syrup
2 eggs
2½ cups crushed bran
  flakes

1 cup sour cream
1 cup flour
1 teaspoon baking soda

Beat syrup and eggs until well blended. Beat in bran flakes and let stand for 5 minutes. Using a wooden spoon, beat in sour cream. Stir in flour and baking soda, mixing just until flour is moistened. Batter will be lumpy. Spoon into greased muffin tins and bake at 400° for about 20 minutes or until lightly browned. Remove from pan and serve hot.   *Makes 12.*

MAPLE OATMEAL MUFFINS

Helen refrigerates leftover muffin batter and can make fresh "from-scratch" muffins for snacks or lunch in the time it takes to bake them.

1 egg, beaten
1 cup milk
¼ cup shortening,
  melted
¾ cup soft maple sugar
1½ cups flour

1 teaspoon baking
  powder
¾ teaspoon salt (or to
  taste)
1¼ cups rolled oats
¼ to ½ cup raisins
  (optional)

Stir together egg, milk, shortening, and maple sugar. Mix flour, baking powder, and salt together and add to egg mixture. Stir in rolled oats until just blended. Add raisins if desired. Spoon into greased muffin tins and bake at 400°-425° for 15 to 20 minutes.   *Makes 12 large muffins.*

GRAHAM BREAD

Maple syrup gives this bread a unique flavor.

1 cup sour milk	3 cups graham flour
1 cup sweet milk	1 teaspoon baking soda
1 cup maple syrup	1 teaspoon salt
⅔ cup all-purpose flour	

Combine all ingredients and bake in a greased and floured 9x5-inch loaf pan at 350° for 50 to 60 minutes. *Makes 1 loaf.*

MARJORIE THURBER'S HOME BAKED BEANS

These very sweet beans can be made in a crock pot as well. Sprinkle sugar over the pork to make a glaze, or bake uncovered for the last half hour to brown the top.

1 pound yellow eye or pea beans	2 teaspoons dry mustard
1 tablespoon baking soda	½ cup catsup
1 teaspoon salt	Salt pork
1 cup maple syrup	

Soak beans overnight. Bring beans to a boil, covered, watching closely so they don't boil over. Turn off stove and let beans stand covered 1 hour. During this time add baking soda. After the 1 hour, bring to boil again and boil until tender. Drain beans, reserving liquid. Add salt, syrup, mustard, catsup, and pork, and enough reserved bean broth to keep beans covered. Bake, covered, in slow oven for 6 to 8 hours. Check and taste periodically to make sure they don't dry out and to add more syrup if necessary. *Serves 8.*

267

SWEET POTATO-MAPLE-APPLE CASSEROLE

Use a good baking apple, like McIntosh or Cortland, that will hold up well during cooking.

1 can (32 ounces) sweet
   potatoes, sliced
   lengthwise, or 4 cups
   sliced sweet potatoes
2 cups apple slices,
   peeled, and cut ¼-
   inch thick

¾ cup maple syrup
¼ cup butter, melted
1 teaspoon salt

Place potato slices in a greased casserole dish. Arrange apple slices on top. Combine syrup, butter, and salt, and pour over potatoes and apples. Cover and bake at 350° for 45 minutes. Uncover and continue baking until apples are tender. Basting improves the flavor; add more maple syrup if desired.

Serves 6-8.

"MY BREAD PUDDING"

This recipe was a favorite of Bertha Robb's mother-in-law, Christine, who had a spoonful of maple syrup on her cereal every morning, and lived to be 94.

3 cups crumbs from
   stale bread, biscuits,
   or cake (preferably a
   combination of all
   three)
Milk to cover

1 egg
½ cup maple sugar
½ teaspoon nutmeg
½ teaspoon salt
½ teaspoon vanilla
½ cup raisins

Place crumbs in 1-quart baking dish and add milk to cover. Let stand to soak about 1 hour. Beat egg and combine with sugar, nutmeg, salt, and vanilla. Add to soaked crumbs along with

(Cont'd)

more warm milk if necessary to make the mixture soft. Add raisins. Bake for 1 hour at 325°, stirring occasionally. Serve with whipped cream or sauce of your choice. *Serves 8.*

POOR FOLK'S PLUM PUDDING

Serve this with a topping of whipped cream or foamy sauce.

1 cup flour
½ cup Indian meal
  (cornmeal)
⅓ cup maple syrup
1 cup cold water
½ cup each raisins and
  English currants

1 teaspoon baking soda,
  dissolved in 2
  teaspoons hot water
½ teaspoon salt

Combine all ingredients and pour into well-greased top of double boiler. Cover and cook over boiling water for 2½ hours, taking care that water boils continuously. *Serves 6.*

MILDRED PRESTON
&
JANICE PRESTON STAFFORD
Richmond, Vermont

Mildred Preston and her daughter Janice Stafford are a double-barreled culinary force in Richmond, Vermont. They frequently entertain large groups of friends and relatives, and both have been active in the restoration of the town's famous Round Church, using their cooking skills to help raise money for the lovely old building.

You would expect that the two women, being so closely related and so fond of each other, would tend to cook the same things or in the same way, but not necessarily so. "I usually plan the menus," says Mildred, "but Janice has ideas of her own! And we don't make everything alike — even basic things like pie crust and gravy we do differently. Janice puts butter in the top of her pies and I usually don't. Janice rolls her pie crusts between sheets of waxed paper but I roll mine on marble. She uses a pastry cutter to mix her pie crust and I use my fingers."

"And," chimes in Janice, "Mother adds cold water to her gravy while I add hot. My gravy gets lumpy if I use cold water, but Mother's doesn't."

It is not unusual for Janice or Mildred to invite thirty or forty guests to the farm, and Mildred once put on a full-scale New England boiled dinner for fifty. "We help each other entertain," Janice explains. "That way we get to go to both parties!"

271

CRANBERRY SALAD

Unmold onto a bed of lettuce leaves, and swirl a dressing of half mayonnaise and half sour cream over the top — perfect for a party.

2 cups raw cranberries	1 cup hot water
1 orange, seeded	1 cup celery, minced
1 cup sugar	Pinch of salt
Juice of ½ lemon	
1 package (3 ounces) lemon gelatin	

Grind cranberries and orange, using a coarse blade. Add sugar and lemon juice and let mixture stand. Dissolve gelatin in hot water and stir in cranberry mixture, celery, and salt. Pour into a 4-cup mold or bowl and chill. When firm, unmold if desired.

Serves 8.

JEANNE DUBE'S WALTERSPIEL (Potato Soup)

A thick, hearty, main-dish soup to take the chill off any winter's day. Serve hot with fresh yeast rolls sliced and browned in butter. Although it is still flavorful reheated the next day, it begins to thicken even more as the potatoes cook down.

4 slices lean bacon, diced	2 egg yolks
6 leeks, thinly sliced	1 cup sour cream
¼ cup chopped onion	1 tablespoon minced parsley
2 tablespoons flour	1 tablespoon minced chervil
4 cups chicken broth	
3 large potatoes, thinly sliced (about 3 cups)	

Sauté bacon in a deep saucepan for 5 minutes, or until nearly

(Cont'd)

crisp. Add leeks and onion, and sauté for another 5 minutes. Stir in flour. Add broth slowly, stirring constantly. Add potatoes and simmer for 1 hour. Combine egg yolks and sour cream, and stir into soup. Simmer for 10 minutes, stirring constantly. Add parsley and chervil. *Serves 8.*

MILDRED'S CHOWDER

Both salt pork and bacon are used to flavor this unique seafood-and-corn chowder. Stir it slowly and gently while cooking so as not to break up the fish too much, and never let it boil.

2-inch-thick piece of salt pork	1 can niblet corn
2 slices bacon	½ pint heavy cream
1 pound haddock fillets	1 quart milk (or enough
4 to 5 potatoes	to achieve desired
4 medium onions	consistency)
2 cans minced clams	Salt and pepper to
1 can small shrimp (broken)	taste

Dice salt pork and bacon, and brown slowly until fat is rendered. Meanwhile, cook haddock fillets in water to cover; when cooked, lift out with a slotted spatula and set aside. Peel and dice potatoes, and cook in the strained fish cooking water. Peel and chop onions, and add to the cooked bacon and salt pork. Cook slowly until onions are transparent. Combine fish, cooked potatoes and cooking water, onions, salt pork, and bacon in a heavy soup pot. Add minced clams, small shrimp, and niblet corn. Gently stir in heavy cream and add enough milk to give chowder desired consistency. Add salt and pepper to taste, and heat through but do not boil. *Serves 8-10.*

BETTY RAND BASSETT'S SPINACH BARS

Cheesey and quiche-like, with a delicious crunchy brown crust top and bottom — great for Sunday brunch. Broccoli may be substituted for the spinach.

4 tablespoons butter
3 eggs
1 cup flour
1 cup milk
½ to 1 teaspoon salt
1 teaspoon baking
   powder
1 pound cheddar
   cheese, grated

1 package (10 ounces)
   frozen chopped
   spinach, thawed and
   drained
1 small onion, chopped
½ cup chopped
   mushrooms (optional)

In a 13x9-inch pan, melt the butter. Mix remaining ingredients together and spoon into pan. Bake at 350° for 30 to 35 minutes. Cool slightly before cutting into squares. Can be served hot or at room temperature.   *Serves 8.*

PAT HEINRICH'S MUSTARD SAUCE

Excellent with ham or New England boiled dinner.

1 small can dry
   mustard
1 cup vinegar

2 eggs
1 cup sugar

Mix mustard and vinegar together in a glass bowl (do not use a metal bowl) and let stand in refrigerator overnight. Place the mixture in the top of an enameled or glass double boiler and beat in eggs and sugar. Cook over boiling water for 20 minutes, beating occasionally with an electric mixer at medium speed. Store in a glass jar (do not use a metal top).

Makes about 1½ cups.

JETTA SWIAT'S CHICKEN DIVAN

Tender chicken breasts surrounded with a bubbling creamy sauce and topped with browned buttered crumbs. Serve with saffron-flavored rice or pilaf mixed with mushrooms and pimiento.

3 packages (10 ounces each) frozen broccoli spears, thawed enough to separate

3 to 4 whole chicken breasts (allow ½ breast per serving), boned

2 cans cream of chicken soup

1 cup mayonnaise

1 teaspoon lemon juice

½ teaspoon curry powder

6 ounces sharp cheddar cheese, grated

½ to 1 cup bread crumbs, buttered

Grease a 13x9-inch baking dish and place broccoli spears on the bottom. Place chicken breasts on top of the broccoli. Combine soup, mayonnaise, lemon juice, and curry powder to make a sauce and pour over chicken. Top with grated cheese and bread crumbs. Bake at 325° for about 1½ hours.

Serves 6-8.

HARRIET RIGGS' DATE COOKIES

A good tea cookie. Watch carefully during baking to prevent burning.

Dough:

¾ cup shortening	3 cups flour
2 cups light brown sugar, packed	1 teaspoon cream of tartar
2 eggs	1 teaspoon baking soda
1 teaspoon vanilla	

Cream shortening and brown sugar; stir in eggs and vanilla, and beat well. Combine flour, cream of tartar, and baking soda, and add to egg mixture. Chill dough for 45 minutes. Roll dough into a long strip 5 inches wide and spread with the filling (below). Roll up dough lengthwise (like a jelly roll) and cut crosswise into 3 sections. Wrap each section in waxed paper and chill for several hours, or freeze. To bake, cut cookies into ⅜-inch slices, and bake at 375° for 8 to 10 minutes.

Filling:

1 package chopped dates	½ cup sugar
1 cup chopped walnuts or pecans	½ cup water

Combine all ingredients and cook until mixture thickens, about 5 to 8 minutes. Cool, spread on cookie dough, and proceed as directed. *Makes 6 dozen.*

MILDRED'S RASPBERRY PIE

One of the world's finest perfumes is the aroma of a raspberry pie baking in the oven. Mildred makes her pies from the home-grown raspberries she and Janice pick each summer. "We have so many berries that we're constantly making pies, jams, and other things and putting the excess in the freezer for winter."

2 cups flour	1 quart raspberries
1 teaspoon salt	1 generous cup sugar
¼ cup cold water	1 heaping teaspoon
1 cup shortening ("I use	flour
Fluffo, when I can	2 tablespoons heavy
find it")	cream

Prepare crust by combining 2 cups flour and salt. Remove ⅓ cup of mixture, combine with cold water, and set aside. Add shortening to remaining flour mixture and mix together until dough forms small pea-sized lumps. Add flour and water mixture, and mix with hands until combined. Divide dough in half, roll out crusts, and line pie plate with bottom crust.

Combine raspberries, sugar, and 1 teaspoon flour; stir together gently and heap into pie shell. Cover with top crust, crimp, and seal; cut vents in top. Spread heavy cream on top and bake for 1 hour at 350°, until pie bubbles up. *Serves 8.*

MARION & ADA URIE
Northeast Kingdom, Vermont

In the Vermont farming valley that spans parts of Craftsbury, Glover, and South Albany, Ada and Marion Urie are a well-known team of excellent cooks. Marion is Ada's daughter, and between them the two women have mastered the art of country cooking, adding a few new twists of their own in the process. No holiday festivity or church supper would be complete without Ada's breads or carrot casserole, or Marion's pies, Scandinavian rolls, or maple butternut fudge.

In her breads, Ada uses whole milk, shortening, sugar, salt, and eggs. She takes great care in shaping the loaves and making the tops smooth and shiny. She cools the baked loaves under a linen cloth because she prefers a soft crust on her bread.

Marion collects the butternuts for her fudge from an old tree on her mother's farm. They look like stewed prunes in the shell and are notoriously hard to extract in one piece. She has a grindstone on the edge of her stove on which she cracks the nuts with a hammer, hitting them just right so they split and she can dig the nut out.

Ada is an organized and meticulous cook, and she has passed these traits on to Marion, who in turn has taught her own daughter the same way.

MARION'S SCANDINAVIAN ROLLS

These light rolls are a marvelous variation of the traditional sweet roll, and the ease of preparation — no kneading and only one rising — is a real plus.

4 cups flour	1 egg, beaten
1 teaspoon salt	1 cup milk, scalded
¼ cup sugar	and cooled
1 cup butter or	Butter
margarine	Sugar
1 tablespoon dry yeast	Cinnamon
¼ cup warm water	

Sift flour, salt, and sugar together. Cut in butter. Dissolve yeast in warm water, and add egg and milk. Blend with dry ingredients. Refrigerate overnight. Divide dough in half; roll each half into a large rectangle. Spread with soft butter and sprinkle generously with sugar and cinnamon. Roll up each rectangle and slice each into 12 rolls. Let rolls rise about 1 hour. Bake at 350° for 15 to 20 minutes, or until nicely browned. Remove from oven and spread with a confectioners sugar glaze flavored with almond extract. Serve warm or cold.

Makes 24 rolls.

COTTAGE CHEESE DILL BREAD

Ada gets a number of requests to make this wonderfully flavorful bread. The recipe makes 6 small loaves, so extras could be frozen or given away as gifts.

2 packages dry yeast	2 tablespoons butter
½ cup warm water	1 scant tablespoon salt
2 cups cottage cheese	½ cup milk
¼ cup sugar	½ teaspoon baking soda
¼ cup dill seed	2 eggs, beaten
1 small onion, grated	5 to 6 cups flour

Dissolve yeast in warm water. In saucepan, heat cheese, sugar, dill, onion, butter, salt, and milk to lukewarm. Add dissolved yeast, soda, and beaten eggs, and beat well. Add 1½ cups flour and beat with electric mixer. Add remaining flour, enough to make a firm dough. Turn onto floured board and knead well. Let rise in oiled bowl until doubled. Knead again and shape into 6 small loaves to fit 6x3¼-inch loaf pans. Let rise and bake 5 minutes at 400°. Reduce heat to 350° and bake 20 to 25 minutes.   *Makes 6 small loaves.*

ADA'S CARROT CASSEROLE

A fine dish for Saturday lunch or Sunday supper, served with a Waldorf salad.

2 tablespoons butter, cut in small pieces	2 cups grated cheese
2 cups mashed carrots	1 small onion, grated
3 eggs, beaten	Salt and pepper
	Paprika

Combine all ingredients, mixing well to blend. Turn into greased 1½-quart casserole dish and bake at 325° for 40 minutes.   *Serves 6.*

ADA'S BAKED INDIAN PUDDING

Ada suggests using a double boiler to cook the cornmeal mixture.
Serve warm with whipped cream.

2 cups milk	½ cup maple syrup
½ cup cornmeal	½ teaspoon ginger
1 egg, beaten	1 teaspoon cinnamon
⅓ cup sugar	1 cup milk

Scald 1¾ cups milk, saving ¼ cup to moisten cornmeal. Stir cornmeal and reserved ¼ cup milk into scalded milk. Stir until thickened and cook 5 minutes. Add beaten egg, sugar, syrup, and spices mixed together. Cook a few minutes. Add 1 cup cold milk and beat well. Pour into well-greased 2-quart casserole dish, set in pan of hot water, and bake slowly (275°-300°), stirring several times, for 2 hours. *Serves 4-6.*

MARION'S RASPBERRY PIE

Divine. Be sure to build the rim of the pie crust high enough so the filling won't overflow into the oven. If using frozen, sweetened berries, reduce sugar to half a cup.

Crust:

1⅓ cups flour	½ cup shortening
½ teaspoon salt	Water

Combine flour and salt in bowl. Cut in shortening until finely blended. Add just enough cold water to make a soft dough. Roll out half of dough for lower crust and other half for top.

Filling:

3 to 4 cups raspberries, fresh or frozen	2 to 3 tablespoons tapioca
1¼ cups sugar (if using fresh berries)	

(Cont'd)

Mix berries, sugar, and tapioca together, and pour into crust.
Cover with top crust. Bake at 400° for 40 minutes.

Serves 10-12.

MARION'S MAPLE BUTTERNUT FUDGE

One of Marion's popular holiday treats is this smooth, fine-grained candy. Use walnuts if butternuts aren't available.

2 cups sugar	2 tablespoons butter
1 cup maple syrup	½ cup butternuts
1 cup milk	

Boil sugar, syrup, and milk together until mixture reaches 235°.
Pour into bowl to cool. Add butter and stir until a grain
shows in the fudge. Add nuts and pour quickly into a buttered
8-inch square pan.

Makes 24 small pieces.

HILDUR WEEDEN
East Killingly, Connecticut

"I've been baking beans on Saturday for as many Saturdays as I've been married," says Hildur Weeden, who was married in 1920, more than 3,000 Saturdays ago. She invariably makes them for Saturday night suppers at home to accompany baked ham, and she follows the country custom of serving them cold after church on Sunday. For decades Hildur's beans have been in steady demand at Eastern Star dinners, church suppers, and local fund-raising drives. Her cooking is classic New England cooking, flavored with Swedish extracts and refined by a lifetime of practice.

Hildur has prepared every family Thanksgiving dinner since 1920, and she sets a lavish—even groaning—table. She roasts turkey and other fowl and red meats using a unique method that includes rubbing a mixture of herbs into the meat and roasting it with eight prunes and some water in the bottom of the pan. The resulting gravy has a beautiful rich color and flavor, and her family members practically fight over the plump roasted prunes.

Holidays wouldn't be complete at Hildur's without raisin-filled cookies, cream puffs, spritz cookies, and fudge. "I make three or four batches of fudge for Halloween and put the dish on the table. The children help themselves to several pieces. Some of the kids I remember from years ago are now grown up and married, but they still come back—and bring along their own children!"

BAKED BEANS

If practice does make perfect, then the baked beans that Hildur has made thousands of times must be nearing perfection. They are sweet, well-browned, and thick, and she always makes them with red kidney beans and Grandma's Molasses—"no other brand will do."

1 pound red kidney
  beans
1 teaspoon salt
⅓ cup sugar (granulated
  or brown)
4 tablespoons catsup
3 tablespoons
  Grandma's Molasses

1 teaspoon dry
  mustard
1 piece salt pork about
  1½-inch square,
  scored

Soak beans overnight in water to cover. In the morning, pour the water off, cover with fresh water, add the salt, and boil until beans are soft. Drain beans in a colander. Place beans in a bean pot or casserole, add water to cover, and add rest of ingredients, stirring well. Bake uncovered at 400° until beans are brown on top (about half an hour), then cover and bake at 350° about 2 hours longer. *Serves 6.*

ROAST CHICKEN, TURKEY, BEEF, LAMB, OR PORK

Hildur's mother, who emigrated from Sweden around the turn of the century, gave this recipe to her daughter years ago. Hildur uses it for roasting all kinds of meat, including the Thanksgiving turkey.

½ teaspoon sugar
1 teaspoon salt
½ teaspoon celery seed
⅛ teaspoon sweet basil
(for beef, lamb, or
pork), or ⅛ teaspoon
sage (for chicken or
turkey)

8 prunes
½ onion
Meat for roasting

Combine seasonings in a small bowl. Wash and dry the meat. Rub the seasonings onto the meat; for chicken or turkey, also rub some inside the bird. Place meat on a roasting rack in a large pan and place prunes around it. Add water and half an onion to help make the gravy brown and tasty. Roast meat uncovered until tender, making sure water does not boil away. Serve the prunes as a treat and use the juice for gravy.

CREAM PUFFS

A showy dessert requiring little work. Great fun for a birthday party or a festive dinner. Top with chocolate sauce, if desired.

1 stick butter	4 eggs
1 cup water	Cream Puff Filling
1 cup flour	(recipe follows)
Dash of salt	

Put butter and water in a saucepan. Place over low heat until mixture boils. Add flour and salt all at once and cook until thick and smooth, stirring constantly. Remove from heat and add unbeaten eggs, one at a time, mixing thoroughly after each addition. Place dough in mounds about 1½ inches apart on a greased baking sheet and bake at 400° about 35 minutes, until puffed and golden. To fill, cut horizontally with a sharp knife. Fill with Cream Puff Filling or with whipped cream. *Makes 12 puffs.*

CREAM PUFF FILLING

½ cup sugar	3 egg yolks
5 tablespoons flour	3 egg whites, stiffly
⅛ teaspoon salt	beaten
¼ cup cold milk	1 teaspoon vanilla
1½ cups milk, scalded	

Mix sugar, flour, and salt together with cold milk and pour slowly into scalded milk. Add egg yolks and cook in a double boiler until thickened. Fold in stiffly beaten egg whites. Cool and add vanilla.

OLD-FASHIONED RAISIN-FILLED COOKIES

Similar to a sugar cookie, but with a tart/sweet filling inside.
Loved by children and adults alike.

Filling:

2 cups chopped raisins	1 tablespoon lemon
⅔ cup sugar	juice
⅔ cup water	1 tablespoon butter

Cook raisins with sugar and water for 10 to 15 minutes, or
until thick, stirring occasionally. Remove from heat and add
lemon juice and butter. Let cool while preparing dough.

Cookie Dough:

1 cup sugar	3 teaspoons baking
1 cup butter or	powder
margarine	¼ teaspoon salt
1 egg, beaten	⅓ cup milk
3 cups sifted flour	2 teaspoons vanilla

Cream sugar and butter; add egg and mix well. Combine
flour, baking powder, and salt, and add alternately to sugar
mixture with milk and vanilla extract. Roll out a portion of
the dough to ⅛-inch thickness and cut into rounds with a
biscuit cutter. Place a teaspoonful of filling on the center of a
round, then cover with another round and press edges together.
Bake at 350° until golden brown (10 to 15 minutes).

Makes 3 dozen.

SPRITZ COOKIES

Elegant when made with a cookie press, but just as tasty shaped into balls. Perfect for the holidays.

1 cup butter
¾ cup sugar
1 egg
2¼ cups all-purpose
  flour
½ teaspoon baking
  powder

Dash of salt
1½ teaspoons almond
  extract (or vanilla
  extract, if desired)

Cream butter and sugar until well mixed. Add unbeaten egg and mix thoroughly. Add flour, baking powder, and salt, and mix well. Stir in almond extract. Fill a cookie press with the dough. Form the cookies on an ungreased cookie sheet. Bake at 350° for 10 to 12 minutes, or until lightly browned.

Makes about 3-4 dozen.

BROWNIES

Moist, with a cake-like texture. Serve plain, frosted, or topped with ice cream.

2 squares unsweetened
  chocolate
⅓ cup butter or
  margarine
⅔ cup flour
⅛ teaspoon baking
  powder

½ teaspoon salt
2 eggs
1 cup sugar
2 teaspoons vanilla
½ cup chopped nuts

Melt chocolate and butter over hot water. Mix flour, baking powder, and salt together. Beat eggs well and gradually beat in sugar. Add chocolate mixture and vanilla to eggs, mixing well, and add flour mixture and nuts. Spread in a greased 8-inch-

(Cont'd)

square pan. Bake for 25 minutes at 350° (do not overbake). Cool and cut into small squares.   *Makes 12-14.*

OLD-FASHIONED RICE PUDDING

An old-time favorite that can be served hot or cold.

¼ cup rice, uncooked	½ cup raisins
1 quart milk	½ teaspoon nutmeg
½ cup sugar	1 teaspoon vanilla
¼ teaspoon salt	2 eggs, lightly beaten

Combine all ingredients, place in a well-buttered baking dish, and place baking dish in a pan of hot water. Bake uncovered at 350° for 2 or 3 hours, stirring every 30 minutes for first 2 hours. Bake until rice is soft.   *Serves 4-5.*

HALLOWEEN FUDGE

Kids from miles around appear at Hildur's house on Halloween, looking for this treat that they've come to expect.

1 tablespoon butter	1 teaspoon vanilla
2 cups sugar	½ cup chopped
⅔ cup milk	walnuts, or 1 heaping
2 squares unsweetened	tablespoon peanut
chocolate	butter (optional)

Melt butter in a heavy saucepan. Add sugar, milk, and chocolate, and stir constantly until chocolate is melted. Boil for 13 minutes and remove from heat. Add vanilla (and walnuts or peanut butter) and beat until creamy and mixture begins to sugar slightly around the edge of the pan. Pour at once into a buttered pan, cool slightly, and mark into squares.

Makes about 64 small squares.

FLUFFY SPONGE CAKE

Makes a high, light cake that can be presented in so many ways. Serve with chocolate sauce and whipped cream, or use for strawberry shortcake. It could also be topped with a mixture of crushed pineapple, beaten egg white, and whipped cream, garnished with a cherry or strawberry.

1½ cups flour	1½ teaspoons vanilla or
6 eggs	almond extract
1½ cups sugar	1½ teaspoons baking
6 tablespoons cold	powder
water	¼ teaspoon salt

Sift flour once before measuring. Separate the egg whites. Beat egg yolks until thick and lemon colored. Beat in sugar gradually. Blend in water and flour alternately. Add vanilla or almond extract and mix thoroughly. Beat egg whites until they almost hold a peak, then add baking powder and salt, and beat until they hold a point. Fold whites into egg yolk mixture. Pour into greased 9-inch tube pan and bake at 350° for 30 to 40 minutes. When done, remove from oven, invert pan on rack, and allow to cool. *Serves 12.*

GINGERBREAD

Dark and spicy, with a reputation as the very best ever.

½ cup shortening
½ cup sugar
1 egg, beaten
1 cup Grandma's
  Molasses
2½ cups flour
1½ teaspoons baking
  soda

½ teaspoon ginger
  (more if desired)
1 teaspoon cinnamon
½ teaspoon ground
  cloves
½ teaspoon salt
1 cup hot water
  (or a little less)

Cream shortening and sugar until light and fluffy. Add beaten egg and molasses, and mix well. Sift together dry ingredients and add, mixing well. Add hot water and beat until smooth. Bake in a greased 9-inch square shallow pan for 25 minutes at 350°, or until done. Serve with whipped cream. *Serves 10-12.*

SUE WELLWOOD
Sharon, New Hampshire

Foremost among Sue Wellwood's interests is herbs,
and she has three different herb gardens around her house to
keep her interest alive. The specimen garden has examples of
many different types of herbs, arranged in a pleasant design. It
is a living catalogue of medicinal, culinary, and decorative
herbs. The Colonial garden contains herbs that would have
appeared in a typical Colonial garden 250 years ago. "I can't
honestly recommend the traditional folk-medicine uses for these
plants," Sue says, "but even if they don't cure, at least they
don't hurt." And the culinary garden, in the dooryard near the
kitchen, is well stocked with edible herbs, both perennial and
annual.

"The joy of herbs," Sue explains, "is that you never
have a dull diet. They have no calories, no bad effects — just
good taste. They enhance foods without being overpowering.
As I got more familiar with the flavors of various herbs, I got
more daring, and started to experiment. It's a matter of choice
— most herbs go with anything."

About the time Sue began using herbs extensively in
cooking, she also began to turn toward a type of cuisine that
relied more and more on whole grains, vegetables, tofu,
chicken, and fish, and less on red meat, butter, cream, salt,
sugar, and other high-cholesterol foods. And if appearance is
any indicator, she is living proof of the healthfulness of her
cooking, for she has a bloom and vitality like that of the herbs
in her garden.

GRANOLA

A dry, unsweetened, fine-textured granola, especially tasty with fresh or dried fruit. Be sure to use raw wheat germ instead of the kind that comes toasted; otherwise it will brown too quickly.

6 cups rolled oats (not pre-cooked)	½ cup sunflower seeds
1 cup raw bran	½ cup sesame seeds
1 cup raw wheat germ	1 cup chopped almonds
½ cup whole wheat flakes	1 cup unsweetened coconut

Combine all ingredients and spread in a thin layer on cookie sheets. Bake at 350° for 10 to 12 minutes, or until lightly toasted. Repeat until all granola is baked. Store in canister or jar with tight-fitting lid. Add raisins, dates, chopped dried pineapple, or apricots if desired, after baking.

Makes about 12 cups.

TOMATO PICK-ME-UP

Serve this in mugs as a beverage or in small chowder bowls, sprinkled with snipped parsley and lemon rind.

1 quart homemade chicken broth	1 large bay leaf
1 can (46 ounces) tomato juice	3 sprigs fresh oregano, or ⅛ to ¼ teaspoon dried
6 sprigs fresh basil, or ¼ to ½ teaspoon dried	Juice of 2 lemons
	⅓ cup vermouth

Heat broth, tomato juice, herbs, and lemon juice to boiling. Add vermouth and simmer until serving time. Remove bay leaf.

Makes about 5½ cups.

HERB OMELET

"You can't let your annual herbs go to seed too early, or they'll stop growing. They're also not as tasty after they've blossomed, so I pull off any buds as soon as I see them. I harvest herbs all summer long, for immediate eating or for drying and freezing."

4 eggs, separated
3 tablespoons milk or
   cream
2 teaspoons raw bran
Dash of black pepper
Salt (optional)
2 teaspoons butter

1½ tablespoons fresh
   herbs — a
   combination of
   chives, parsley, basil,
   thyme, chervil, or
   your favorite
   mixture — snipped
   fine with scissors

Beat egg yolks until thick and light yellow. Add cream, bran, pepper, and salt if desired, and mix thoroughly. Beat egg whites until stiff. Combine, folding yolk mixture into egg whites. Melt butter in omelet pan or frying pan and pour in egg mixture. ("I use a divided omelet pan and put half of the butter and half of the eggs into each pan.") When omelet is nearly set, add mixed herbs and fold over. Cook until done. Slip omelet onto a heated serving platter. *Serves 4.*

TABOULI

A Middle-Eastern salad which could also be served at a party as an appetizer.

1 cup boiling water
1 cup bulgur
2 to 3 tomatoes, diced
1 green pepper, diced
1 cucumber, peeled
and diced
1 to 2 celery stalks,
diced
4 to 5 radishes, diced
¼ cup snipped parsley
½ cup snipped mint
leaves

½ cup fresh lemon or
lime juice, or a
combination
¼ cup oil ("I use a cold-
pressed, blended
oil")
⅓ cup chopped onion
or scallion
1 to 2 teaspoons (sea)
salt, or to taste

Pour boiling water over bulgur and let set 1 hour. Drain off any unabsorbed water. Combine other ingredients with bulgur. Toss gently and chill. Serve on a bed of lettuce, garnished with tomato wedges and additional parsley.

Serves 4-5.

GAZPACHO

The addition of bread to her gazpacho came by circumstance, not design, says Sue: "It started accidentally when I absent-mindedly threw croutons into the blender while I was talking to someone. Everyone liked the result, and I've been using bread in gazpacho ever since."

6 medium tomatoes,
  peeled and chopped
2 stalks celery,
  chopped
1 medium red onion,
  chopped
1 medium white
  onion, chopped
2 medium cucumbers,
  peeled and chopped
1 green pepper,
  chopped
1 carrot, grated
1 garlic clove, chopped

4 cups whole-grain
  bread, coarsely
  broken
4 cups water
¼ cup vinegar or
  lemon juice
2 teaspoons (sea) salt,
  or to taste
3 tablespoons olive oil
½ to ¾ cup mixed fresh
  herbs: basil, chervil,
  chives, parsley, salad
  burnet, tarragon,
  thyme

Combine all ingredients and mix gently. Puree in blender, doing a small amount at a time. Cover and chill for several hours or overnight. At serving time, garnish with any of the following: croutons, snipped parsley, chives, diced green pepper, cucumber, or tomato.

Serves 8.

MACARONI SALAD

An attractive summer dish to serve at a cookout or take on a picnic.

1¼ cups uncooked macaroni ("I use macaroni made from artichoke flour")
Juice of 1 lemon
½ cup chopped celery
¼ cup chopped green pepper
3 tablespoons chopped pimiento
1¼ cups cubed cheddar cheese
3 tablespoons snipped fresh chives
¼ cup chopped fresh parsley
2 to 4 teaspoons dried dill, or 2 to 4 tablespoons fresh
1 cup cooked green peas
2 cups cooked salad shrimp
½ cup mayonnaise

Cook macaroni according to directions on package. Drain. Add remaining ingredients and mix lightly. Chill for several hours or overnight. Serve on a bed of crisp lettuce, bordered with tomato wedges, slices of hard-cooked eggs, ripe olives, and lemon wedges. *Serves 6-8.*

SCALLOP SALAD

Out of this world! The green of the peas and fresh herbs combined with the red pimiento make this a lovely dish for luncheon or a special summer supper. Sauté the scallops in butter until tender, then proceed as directed.

1 pound cooked scallops, cut into bite-size pieces (unless using small bay scallops)
1 cup diced cooked potatoes
1 cup cooked peas
3 tablespoons lemon juice
1 tablespoon minced onion
1 tablespoon snipped chives
1 tablespoon snipped fresh basil
1 tablespoon chopped pimiento
½ cup mayonnaise, or more if desired
½ to 1 teaspoon (sea) salt
Dash of freshly ground black pepper

Combine all ingredients and toss gently. Chill before serving.

Serves 6.

301

SPINACH LASAGNA

A good, hearty lasagna made with fresh spinach and freshly grated Parmesan cheese. Be sure to drain the spinach thoroughly before using.

Sauce:

¾ cup chopped onion
1 garlic clove, minced
2 tablespoons olive oil
½ teaspoon dried thyme
½ teaspoon dried rosemary
1 teaspoon dried basil
1 teaspoon dried oregano
2 tablespoons dried parsley flakes
¼ teaspoon black pepper, or to taste
1 teaspoon (sea) salt, or to taste
1 can (35 ounces) peeled Italian tomatoes
2 small cans tomato paste

Sauté onion and garlic in olive oil. Add other ingredients and simmer for half an hour.

Filling:

4 bags (10 ounces each) fresh spinach, or same amount from your garden
6 to 7 lasagna noodles ("I use noodles made from artichoke flour")
2 to 4 tablespoons dried parsley flakes
2 pounds ricotta cheese or cottage cheese
¾ to 1 pound Parmesan cheese, freshly grated
1 pound mozzarella cheese, sliced

Wash and trim spinach. Steam 1 bag at a time briefly, until wilted. Drain very well, or lasagna will be too juicy. Cook lasagna noodles and drain. Add 1 to 2 tablespoons parsley to

(Cont'd)

each pound of ricotta cheese and mix well.

Assemble layers in a 14x10-inch buttered baking dish in this order:

3 lasagna noodles
½ of the spinach
1 pound ricotta cheese
⅓ of the Parmesan cheese
½ pound mozzarella cheese slices
½ of sauce

Repeat, using an extra noodle if needed. Top with remaining Parmesan cheese. Bake at 375° for 35 to 40 minutes.

Serves 8-10.

BLUEBERRY PUDDING

Experiment with various amounts of mint, lemon rind, and ginger to discover the combination that suits your palate best.

1 quart blueberries	6 slices good-quality
½ cup sugar	white bread
½ cup water	Mint, chopped
2 to 3 tablespoons soft	Lemon rind, grated
butter	Powdered ginger

In a pan, combine blueberries, sugar, and water. Boil for 10 minutes or until berries are soft. Butter bread generously. Put 2 slices of bread in the bottom of a dessert bowl. Sprinkle with chopped mint, grated lemon rind, and powdered ginger. Pour one third of the blueberry mixture over the bread. Repeat twice, omitting the mint, lemon rind, and ginger on the last layer. Run a knife through the pudding several times to help the bread absorb the blueberry juice. Chill for several hours or overnight. Serve plain, with vanilla ice cream, or with whipped cream.

Serves 6-8.

RAYMONDE WOODWARD
East Enosburg, Vermont

"I didn't learn how to cook until I was thirty," says
Raymonde Woodward, "but once I got interested, I kept on
going." Raymonde is a cheerful, energetic, whimsical, and
creative cook, who has always resisted the temptation to serve
her family fast foods, and as a result, foods like crêpes and
homemade French bread are normal fare in the household.
"Our three daughters had to learn from childhood how to eat
an artichoke."

Raymond calls herbs the ABCs of cooking; she grows
a wide variety and uses them in most of her dishes. Instead of
drying herbs for long-term keeping, she freezes them, which
helps retain the flavor and bright color.

The Vermont finalist in a national cooking contest,
Raymonde asserts that "there are no new recipes, just variations
of old recipes, adapted to whatever is on hand. A recipe is like
gossip," she says, "you just keep adding on to it!"

RAISIN AND COTTAGE CHEESE BUNS

Roll the dough up tightly so the filling inside will not spill out when the cylinder of dough is cut into pieces. Serve these nutritious buns warm with a white icing.

1 cup cottage cheese	½ cup white flour
3 tablespoons milk	2 teaspoons baking
1 egg, separated	powder
⅓ cup oil	½ cup raisins
⅓ cup sugar	½ cup chopped nuts
1 cup whole wheat	5 tablespoons sugar
flour	1 tablespoon cinnamon

Mix together cottage cheese, milk, egg yolk, oil, and sugar. Mix flours and baking powder together and add to cottage cheese mixture. Mixture will be sticky. Knead on lightly floured board for only a short time and roll into a 17x8-inch rectangle. Baste with the egg white. Sprinkle with raisins, nuts, sugar, and cinnamon. Roll up to make a long cylinder and cut into 12 pieces. Place in greased pan and bake in 350° oven for about 25 minutes. *Makes 12.*

FRENCH BREAD/ROLLS

"I baste the rolls with ice water after about ten minutes in the oven — it scares them to death, and they get crunchy."

2 cups warm water	1 teaspoon salt
1 teaspoon honey	1 tablespoon oil
1 scant tablespoon	6 cups flour
yeast (1 package dry)	(approximately)
1 tablespoon diastatic	
malt (optional — see	
below)	

Mix water, honey, and yeast together, and let stand until

(Cont'd)

bubbles appear. Add malt if desired, salt, oil, and 2 cups flour. Beat well. Work the rest of the flour in gradually and knead dough for 20 minutes. Cover and let rise for 5 to 12 hours. ("I often start my bread the night before and let it rise overnight.") Punch the dough down, and let rise for another 2 to 4 hours, until doubled. Punch down and shape into 2 loaves or 2 dozen hard rolls (or a combination of both). Let rise for 20 minutes. Bake in a 400° oven for about 10 minutes, baste with ice water to achieve a hard crust, reduce heat to 350°, and bake 20 to 30 minutes longer.

Makes 2 loaves or 2 dozen hard rolls.

Diastatic Malt: In a slow oven, dry ½ cup sprouted wheat kernels, turning a few times, until thoroughly dry. Pulverize in a blender, and store in the refrigerator. The enzymes in the malt help convert starch to sugar.

SNOWPEA AND CARROT SALAD

Colorful, crunchy summertime salad.

2 cups fresh snowpeas, cut diagonally
2 carrots, cut in thin rounds
1 tablespoon lemon juice
3 tablespoons sesame oil
1 teaspoon soy sauce
1 tablespoon sunflower seeds
½ teaspoon chopped mint

Simmer both vegetables in a little water until crisp-tender. Mix the remaining ingredients together; pour over cooked, drained vegetables and stir to blend. Serve either hot or cold. *Serves 4.*

STUFFED ONIONS

It is important to use stale bread in this recipe; otherwise too much liquid will be absorbed and the mixture will not blend together well.

2 stale rolls
½ cup milk, warmed
2 ounces ham, cooked and chopped
2 ounces leftover meat, minced
2 eggs
Chopped parsley, salt, pepper, marjoram to taste

6 to 8 onions
2 tablespoons butter
1 tablespoon bread crumbs
4 tablespoons grated cheese
1 cup beef stock

Soak the stale rolls in warmed milk and squeeze out. Combine the rolls with meats, eggs, and seasonings, and mix well. Peel onions, leaving them whole, and simmer for 20 minutes. Trim the ends, scoop out the centers carefully, and chop the center portion before adding to the meat stuffing. Grease a baking pan with the butter. Stuff the onions and place them in the pan. Sprinkle with crumbs and cheese, and pour stock over the top. Bake for 30 minutes in a 350° oven.   *Serves 4.*

ZUCCHINI PIE

You can use French bread dough for the crust, cutting off enough dough to line an eight-inch pie plate when rolled out thin. Do this after the dough has risen once and been punched down. Do not let it rise again. Or, use your favorite pizza crust or pie crust recipe.

2 cups thinly sliced
  zucchini
1 garlic clove, minced
1 tablespoon oil
1 tablespoon butter
1 tablespoon flour
½ cup milk

1 egg
¼ teaspoon each:
  marjoram, salt, and
  pepper
½ cup shredded cheese
½ tomato, sliced

Sauté the zucchini and garlic in hot oil briefly. Add the butter and flour, and stir for about 5 minutes. Cool. Beat the milk, egg, and spices together, and mix with the zucchini mixture. Line a pie plate with preferred crust, spread the filling over the crust, and top with the shredded cheese. Decorate with tomato slices. Bake at 400° for 25 minutes, or until the crust is golden brown.   *Serves 4.*

PASTA AL FORNO

"This is a nice dish to make ahead of time and you can eat it cold, warm, at midnight — however you wish."

1 medium eggplant, peeled and sliced lengthwise
Olive oil
½ pound ground meat (or leftover meat, minced)
1 small onion, chopped
2 tablespoons chopped fresh oregano, or 1 teaspoon dried
3 to 4 cups tomato sauce (recipe follows)
½ pound spaghetti, cooked al dente
2 cups peas
2 hard-boiled eggs, sliced
3 ounces Genoa salami, thinly sliced and quartered
3 ounces mortadella (donkey sausage), if available
4 ounces mozzarella cheese
2 tablespoons chopped fresh sweet basil, or 1 teaspoon dried
1 cup grated Parmesan or other cheese
2 raw eggs
Black pepper

Soak the eggplant slices in salted water, if desired, for about 20 minutes; rinse and pat dry. Fry in olive oil until golden. Brown the meat in olive oil along with chopped onion and half the oregano. In a deep dish, spread some tomato sauce (recipe follows) in the bottom and begin layering the ingredients, using about half of each: spaghetti, meat, peas, hard-boiled eggs, salami, mortadella, mozzarella cheese, eggplant, basil, grated cheese. Repeat sauce and other ingredients, ending with eggplant. Beat the 2 raw eggs with 1 tablespoon water and pour over the whole works, using a fork to pierce the layers gently and let the egg flow in. Sprinkle with more grated cheese, oregano, and black pepper. Bake, uncovered, for about 40 minutes at 400°. Cut into squares or wedges to serve. Can be served hot or cold.   *Serves 6-8.*

Tomato Sauce:

1 can (6 ounces)
tomato paste
2 cans (1 pound each)
whole tomatoes, or
use fresh if available
2 chicken bouillon
cubes, dissolved in 1
cup boiling water
1 large onion, chopped

8 garlic cloves, minced
1 tablespoon chopped
fresh oregano
3 tablespoons chopped
fresh basil
1 teaspoon mustard
½ teaspoon cinnamon
¼ cup olive oil

Combine all ingredients and simmer for 2 to 5 hours, stirring occasionally. All ingredients are subject to your own liking.

CURRIED CHICKEN

Raymonde's entry in the national chicken-cooking contest incorporates the flavors of sage, mint, and curry.

2 to 3 teaspoons curry
powder
½ teaspoon mint
flakes, crushed
½ teaspoon sage
leaves, crushed
¼ teaspoon salt
2 to 3 teaspoons lemon
juice

1 broiler chicken, cut
up
3 tablespoons oil
½ cup water
1 teaspoon sesame
seeds, toasted

Make a paste of the curry powder, mint, sage, salt, and lemon juice, and spread it over the chicken pieces. Heat the oil in a heavy pan and brown the chicken for about 10 minutes. Drain excess fat. Add water, cover and simmer for 20 minutes. Turn pieces and continue cooking about 15 to 20 minutes longer, until tender. Sprinkle with sesame seeds before serving. *Serves 4.*

CARAMEL CRÈME WITH FRESH RASPBERRIES

Absolutely elegant — brandy lends a gourmet touch, raspberries an exquisite color.

½ cup sugar
2 cups hot milk
4 egg yolks
3 tablespoons
  cornstarch

1 to 2 tablespoons
  brandy
1 cup whipped cream
2 cups fresh
  raspberries

Heat the sugar in a heavy pan until golden and bubbly, being careful not to burn it. Remove the pan from the heat and add hot milk, stirring until the sugar is dissolved. (Return pan to the heat if necessary.) Beat the egg yolks and add the cornstarch. Add a bit of the hot milk to the eggs and then slowly add the eggs to the rest of the hot milk. Cook over low heat, stirring constantly, until mixture thickens and bubbles for 1 minute. Cool. Stir in brandy and chill. Fold in whipped cream just before serving. Fill 6 glasses two thirds full and fill to the top with raspberries. *Serves 6.*

NOTES

INDEX